111 Places
in London
that You
Shouldn't Miss

Photographs by Birgit Weber

emons:

For Helmut

© Emons Verlag GmbH
All rights reserved
© Photographs: Birgit Weber, except chapter 4, 8, 15, 20, 25, 28, 30, 35, 52, 53, 59, 69, 85, 102, 106 (John Sykes)
Design: Eva Kraskes, based on a design
by Lübekke | Naumann | Thoben
Maps: altancicek.design, www.altancicek.de
Printing and binding: Grafisches Centrum Cuno, Calbe
Printed in Germany 2015
ISBN 978-3-95451-346-8
Revised new edition, June 2015

Did you enjoy it? Do you want more?
Join us in uncovering new places around the world on:
www.111places.com

Foreword

In a particularly rainy English summer we pounded miles of wet pavements, visiting well over 111 places and taking more than 8000 photos in order to arrive at the selection presented here.

Famous sights like Big Ben and tourist magnets such as the British Museum are not included, as they have already been described in countless travel guides. We looked at places that visitors might only find on their second or fifth trip to London. Most of them are in inner London, but excursions beyond the city centre to all points of the compass are also included.

We aim to show the breathtaking diversity of a city where all the cultures of the world meet. Its architecture ranges from aristocratic residences to heritage-listed wooden huts, its places of leisure from gentlemen's clubs with strict admission criteria to pubs for everyone, its shops from historic emporiums to stores selling in-your-face young fashion. We invite readers to accompany us to a synagogue, a Hindu temple, a Buddhist pagoda, some churches and an unconsecrated cemetery.

We look at the grave of a king of Corsica in Soho, the wine dealer that kept records of its customers' weight, the spot where pirates were hanged in the river, the subterranean cycle path to Scotland, the high-rise block of flats designed by James Bond's mortal enemy, and a hidden haven for Thames mudlarks.

There is a deliberate gap in the list of 111 places: 110 is followed by 112. Fans of cricket will know the reason for this superstition, and everyone else can read about it in connection with Lord's Cricket Ground (number 53).

We hope those who explore London with this book will enjoy the experience as much as we enjoyed researching, taking photographs and writing it.

John Sykes & Birgit Weber

111 Places

1__Albert Bridge
A frail old soldier

Tower Bridge may be world-famous, but nothing spans the Thames more beautifully than Albert Bridge a few miles upstream. Named after Queen Victoria's consort, the bridge is truly enchanting after dark, when 4000 fairy lights put a magic sparkle on its octagonal towers and iron stays. During daylight hours, the pastel shades of its paint – pink, blue and yellow – pick out the intricacies of the structure. The dainty appearance of Albert Bridge is not misleading: ever since its inauguration in 1873, it has given headaches to civil engineers, as its 19th-century nickname, the »trembling lady«, indicates. The historic signs that warned companies of soldiers from nearby Chelsea Barracks to break step as they marched across are still in place.

The engineer Rowland Mason Ordish designed Albert Bridge as his own patented variant of the cable-stayed bridge. It had to be reinforced only eleven years after opening. In the late 1950s, a vigorous campaign by prominent supporters, including the poet John Betjeman, prevented demolition. For the centenary of the bridge in 1973, piers were placed in the river to shore it up. Recent structural problems are connected to the social make-up of the neighbourhood: residents from the north bank drive across in their heavy, four-wheel-drive »Chelsea tractors«, but the brittle cast-iron structure was never intended to carry motorised traffic. They also walk their poodles to Battersea Park on the south bank. As some dogs cannot wait till they reach the other side, urine corrodes the wooden deck beneath the roadway.

Following restoration, Albert Bridge was reopened in 2011, not by royalty but with »walkies« for Prince and Albert, two residents of Battersea Dogs' Home. A splendid sight but frail with age, like the uniformed veteran soldiers of the nearby Royal Hospital, the bridge stands upright and does its duty.

Address Chelsea Embankment/Cheyne Walk (north side of the bridge) | **Transport** Sloane Square (Circle, District Line); bus 170 from Victoria to Albert Bridge | **Tip** The Royal Hospital in Chelsea with its beautiful chapel and Great Hall was built by Christopher Wren in 1682 (Royal Hospital Road, open Mon–Fri 10am–4pm).

2 The Albert Memorial
A shiny gold prince

London's most elaborate monument honours Albert of Saxe-Coburg and Gotha (1819–61). Cast in bronze and gilded, the husband of Queen Victoria is enthroned in Kensington Gardens beneath a 54-metre-high Gothic canopy. Seated in a pensive pose, his head slightly turned to the left, he looks towards the South Kensington museums rather than the Royal Albert Hall opposite. One hand holds the catalogue of the Great Exhibition of 1851, in which he played a leading role. In the Crystal Palace, a huge structure made of iron and glass, this first-ever world fair presented the triumphs of Western civilisation and above all of Great Britain, the world's leading industrial and colonial power. The profits from the Great Exhibition were used to found the institutions now known as the Victoria & Albert Museum, the Natural History Museum and the Science Museum.

The monument, unveiled in 1876 by Queen Victoria, embodies his faith in progress. Groups of white marble figures on the plinth symbolise industry, commerce, engineering and agriculture. Beneath these stand 169 life-size relief carvings of European writers, painters, composers, architects and engineers, including a solitary woman, Nitocritis of Babylon. A magnificent gilded fence keeps visitors at a distance, but around it sculptural allegories of the four continents can be admired from close up. For all the exotic garments of the human figures, the animals steal the scene: Asia is represented by a friendly-looking elephant, America by an imposing buffalo, Africa by a camel wrinkling its nose. Europe sits on her bull, holding a sceptre as a sign of authority, next to Britannia with a trident, the symbol of sea power. During his lifetime, Albert rejected the idea of being commemorated by a monument, fearing an »artistic monstrosity«. In fact, the architect, George Gilbert Scott, and the sculptors created a masterpiece.

Address Kensington Gardens, south side, SW7 2AP **Transport** Knightsbridge (Piccadilly Line) **Tip** The Cast Court of the Victoria & Albert Museum (daily 10am–5.45pm) is a kind of Disneyland for sculpture, a collection of plaster casts of great works, including Trajan's Column from Rome, cathedral doors and monumental tombs.

3__Apothecaries' Hall
A survival from the age of guilds

In the alleys and courts between Ludgate Hill and the Thames, you can still get a feel of a bygone, small-scale London – for example in narrow Black Friars Lane next to a railway viaduct. The friars were Dominicans, whose refectory became a theatre after the dissolution of the monasteries under King Henry VIII. Shakespeare once trod the boards there, in the place now called Playhouse Yard, and bought a house in nearby Ireland Yard. Another part of the Dominicans' premises was taken over in 1632 by the Society of Apothecaries, one of London's 109 »livery companies«.

The livery companies, so called for their ceremonial gowns, originated in the Middle Ages as guilds of tailors, wine merchants, goldsmiths and other occupations. They laid down the rules of their trades, had religious roles and elected the Lord Mayor. Most of them have now become charitable organisations, but some still have professional functions. The Society of Apothecaries possesses the oldest remaining livery hall. Parts of it, including the 18-metre-long Great Hall with its oak panelling, large chandelier and historic portraits of officers of the society, date from 1670. The coat of arms that adorns the modest façade in Black Friars Lane shows Apollo slaying a dragon, the symbol of disease, with a Latin motto meaning »I am called a bringer of help throughout the world«.

Originally organised within the guild of pepper merchants, the apothecaries founded their own livery company in 1617. Half a century later, they established a botanical garden for growing plants, the Chelsea Physic Garden, which still exists. Past members include the poet John Keats and Elizabeth Garrett Anderson (1836–1917), the first Englishwoman to qualify as a doctor. Until 1922, the Society of Apothecaries ran a pharmaceutical business. Today it holds post-graduate examinations in medicine and awards a prize for medical history. And the senior members still elect the Lord Mayor.

Address Black Friars Lane, EC4V | Transport Blackfriars (Circle, District Line) | Tip As a consolation for the fact that Apothecaries' Hall is rarely open to the public, a nearby pub, The Black Friar on the corner of New Bridge Street, has an opulent interior in the Arts & Crafts style.

APOTHECARIES HALL

4_ The Argyll Arms

A refuge from shopping hell

Pushing and jostling along Oxford Street, Londoners and visitors from all over the world engage in a collective retail frenzy. For those who find this place unbearable, and for fashion victims seeking to recuperate after their shopping trip, there is a haven close to Oxford Circus Tube Station in Argyll Street: a pub that is also a gem of interior design.

In the 18th century, the Duke of Argyll resided in the street – the Palladium Theatre now occupies the site – and the sign over the door bears his coat of arms. A tavern has stood here since 1742, but the wonderful interior of the Argyll Arms dates mainly from 1895. This was the golden age of pub architecture when breweries, facing stiffer competition than ever from other places of amusement such as theatres, bought up modest watering holes and turned them into gleaming palaces. They aimed to counter the arguments of the temperance movement by demonstrating taste and decency.

The Argyll Arms is fitted with dark wood, mirrors and etched glass. Three snug screened-off drinking areas lie between a corridor and the long bar. The partitions are made from carved mahogany and frosted glass into which delicate patterns have been etched: floral motifs, cornucopias and vases. Subdued lamplight glows in the dimness, sparkles in the mirrors and lends depth to the patterns in the glass. Above this, painted dark red, is a ceiling of Lincrusta, a deeply embossed material related to linoleum that was used as a wall covering in Victorian times. This ceiling may well be as old as the building, which dates from 1868. To the rear is a rare surviving example of a publican's office, also partitioned off with panels of etched glass and mahogany, and boasting a clock with a carved encasement. As The Argyll Arms is a listed building, its beauty will be preserved for future generations of drinkers and exhausted shoppers.

Address 18 Argyll Street, W1F 7TP | Transport Oxford Circus (Bakerloo, Central, Victoria Line) | Tip Take the Central Line two stops east to Holborn to admire another fine old pub: The Princess Louise (209 High Holborn) with its tiles, mirrors and a historic gents' toilet.

5_ The Athenaeum Club

The goddess admits those who are worthy

Among the grey stone façades on Pall Mall and St James's Street, the district of gentlemen's clubs, one club stands out from the others thanks to its bright, cream-coloured paint, a replica of the Parthenon frieze in white on a blue background and a brilliantly gilded female figure, the goddess Athene, who stands above the Doric columns of the entrance with her helmet and spear. Her gaze lowered and left arm outstretched, she seems to be inviting deserving mortals into the club.

In 1824 the writer John Wilson Croker, the artist Sir Thomas Lawrence and other eminent men founded the Athenaeum Club, intending it to be a meeting place for outstanding persons in the fields of science, art and literature. Whereas other clubs appealed to army officers, politicians, travellers or gamblers and drinkers, the Athenaeum was a refuge for intellectuals. The decision to spend money on the expensive Parthenon frieze instead of facilities to cool members' drinks underlined its aspirations, as a satirical verse recorded: »I'm John Wilson Croker, I do as I please; instead of an ice house I give you – a frieze!« The members have included Joseph Conrad, Rudyard Kipling, J. M. W. Turner, Charles Darwin and, to date, 52 Nobel Prize laureates. The scientist Michael Faraday, whose wheelchair has been preserved in the club, ensured that the rooms had electric lighting as early as 1886. At the foot of the wide staircase Charles Dickens and William Makepeace Thackeray, the latter mortally ill, were reconciled in 1863 after a quarrel that had lasted for years.

Today government ministers, high-ranking civil servants and bishops are among the members. Women were not admitted until 2002, but now they too can dine and stay overnight in the club, read the 80,000 volumes in the imposing library, invite guests to private occasions, or simply snooze behind a newspaper in a leather armchair beneath the heavily framed portraits in the Morning Room.

Address 107 Pall Mall, SW1Y 5ER | Transport Piccadilly Circus (Bakerloo, Piccadilly Line) | Opening times Unless you can get a member to invite you, forget it! | Tip Many clubs prefer not to be identified by a sign on the door. On a walk along Pall Mall, look out for the Travellers Club at 104 Pall Mall; the Reform Club, no. 106; the Army and Navy Club, no. 36; and the Oxford and Cambridge Club, no. 71.

6__ The Barbican

A monstrosity or a home with culture?

It is said that no-one lives in the City, that square mile within London's historic city wall where more than 300,000 people have their place of work and a mere 12,000 their dwelling. One third of the latter group are at home in The Barbican.

Wartime bombing turned the parish of Cripplegate into an uninhabited field of ruins. In order to breathe life into the City, plans for residential development began in the 1950s, but the project was completed only in the mid-1970s. Some 2000 flats were constructed from raw-looking, dark concrete, many of them in three towers that rise 123 metres with 42 storeys each. The labyrinth of steps and raised walkways that link the 13 residential blocks can be relied upon to confuse visitors. In keeping with the word »Barbican«, meaning outworks of a fortification, the whole complex turns inwards, saluting its surroundings with concrete cliffs. Is it an urban atrocity?

In fact the Barbican has become a popular, traffic-free place to live and in 2001 received the accolade of a Grade II listing as a site of special architectual interest. The closed-off architecture keeps out the roar of London's streets. Residents are soothed by the sound of splashing fountains on the café terrace and the sight of hanging green gardens or water lilies and reeds in the big pond. The Barbican Arts Centre, home to a conservatory filled with 2000 tropical plants, is a respected venue for cinemas, plays, concerts and exhibitions. Tourists find historical sights such as the 1000-year-old church of St Giles-without-Cripplegate. Built in its present form in 1394 and altered many times, it is the church where Oliver Cromwell married and the poet John Milton was laid to rest. Gardens and a moat flank substantial remains of London's medieval city wall with its Roman foundations. As the stone cladding was taken for other purposes, only the core of the wall survives – rough masonry, hardly more attractive than the concrete of the Barbican towers.

Address North of London Wall, EC2Y 8DT | **Transport** Barbican (Circle, Hammersmith & City, Metropolitan Line) | **Opening times** Conservatory usually Sun 11am–5pm, see www.barbican.org.uk | **Tip** South of The Barbican, the historic seat of London's government, Guildhall, stands above the remains of a Roman amphitheatre which, like the hall dating from 1411 and the art gallery, is open to visitors (Mon–Sat 10am–5pm, Sun noon–4pm).

7 _ Belgrave Square
Family property

In previous centuries, the art of making the right marriage often determined the prosperity of aristocratic dynasties. In the case of the Grosvenor family, whose head bears the title Duke of Westminster, a well-chosen bride has been effective to this day. The undeveloped land that came to the Grosvenor estates through a 17th-century heiress is now one of the poshest parts of London: Mayfair, Belgravia and Pimlico. The family has kept hold of this prime land, which makes the sixth Duke of Westminster, born in 1951, the richest man of his class.

A centrepiece of this property portfolio is Belgrave Square. At the north-east corner of the square is a memorial to Robert Grosvenor, under whom the neoclassical rows with their columned entrances and white stucco façades were built in the years up to 1840 on marshy terrain that had been a haunt of highwaymen. The duke's architect, George Basevi, designed a row of eleven or twelve imposing houses on each side of the square. In the corners between these terraces he placed palatial detached houses, and the space in the middle was laid out as a garden. Once the home of the aristocracy and the rich, Belgrave Square now serves mainly as a prestigious address for the embassies of Germany, Portugal, Serbia, Bahrain, Norway and Syria. The Duke of Westminster himself has his town house nearby in Eaton Square, which is named after the family's country seat in Cheshire. His London neighbours include Roman Abramovich and Andrew Lloyd Webber.

Fenced in and screened by shrubs from the prying eyes of passers-by, the gardens in the middle of Belgrave Square are a private space. Once a year, however, during the Open Garden Squares Weekend in June, everyone has an opportunity to stroll where otherwise only the privileged residents are admitted. To gain possession of a key to the gate, you need more than a few million pounds.

Address Belgrave Square, SW1X 8PZ | **Transport** Hyde Park Corner (Piccadilly Line) | **Tip** In Belgrave Mews behind the German embassy, The Star Tavern serves excellent Fullers beer and pub food at prices that normal people can afford.

8_ Berry Bros. & Rudd
Wine merchants for 300 years

The dark green paint on the shop front is the first clue to its age. The windows and doors look as if they have been painted a hundred times without the woodwork ever being sanded down. The surface is covered with little hollows and blisters, and all the corners are rounded, but the paintwork has a deep shine. Inside the shop, oak panelling, dim lighting and the alarming slope of the floor confirm the first impression.

The present building dates from 1731, but a certain Widow Bourne started selling spices, tea and coffee on the site as early as 1698, and soon added wine to her assortment. These origins are displayed by the sign of a grinder over the door and by huge scales for weighing sacks of coffee beans – and customers too. Regulars can still take advantage of this service and have their names entered in a ledger that records the weight of Lord Byron.

In 1810 George Berry took over the business that now bears the names of his sons and a partner, Hugh Rudd, a specialist in German wines. Today Berry Bros. employ five qualified »masters of wine« to advise a discerning clientele. The shop has a separate room for »fine wine reserves«, but anyone can walk in and buy a single bottle at an affordable price. If the desired vintage is not on the shelves, the friendly sales staff will find something suitable among the 20,000 bottles in the cellar.

The longevity of this wine merchant is connected to its prime location in St James's, where the well-to-do gentleman has his essential suppliers. Opposite Berry Bros., Truefitt & Hill sells exquisite shaving accessories. The hat maker Locke, the shoe maker Lobb and Dunhill's cigar shop are close by, and fine shirts can be purchased round the corner in Jermyn Street. For all its air of tradition, Berry Bros. has large modern storehouses outside London and sells online – but to buy their wine in style, only one place will do.

Address 3 St James's Street, SW1A 1EG | Transport Green Park (Piccadilly, Victoria Line) | Opening times Mon–Fri 10am–6pm, Sat 10am–5pm | Tip The Red Lion in Crown Passage between King Street and Pall Mall is a historic pub with lots of atmosphere.

9 Bevis Marks Synagogue

A 300-year-old Jewish community

London's oldest synagogue lies hidden between office blocks. Its inconspicuousness is not only the result of incessant construction work in the City: when it was founded, Jewish places of worship were not allowed to stand directly on a public thoroughfare. In view of the roaring traffic all around, the sheltered location in a courtyard off the street Bevis Marks is a blessing today both for the congregation and for visitors who come to enjoy a historic and architectural jewel.

After a period of 350 years during which it was prohibited to practise the Jewish religion in England, in 1656 Jews who had been expelled from Spain and Portugal, and had worshipped in London discreetly for several years, established a small synagogue in Creechurch Lane near Bevis Marks. Their community flourished and commissioned Joseph Avis, a pupil of Sir Christopher Wren, to build a new synagogue, which was opened in 1701 and has hardly been changed since then.

The most striking features inside are the raised reading desk and the ark, a decorated cupboard on the east wall to hold the torah. The ark is made of painted oak with Corinthian columns and beautiful woodcarving. Seven many-branched chandeliers stand for the days of the week, and the twelve columns supporting the women's gallery symbolise the tribes of Israel. The plain benches at the back are survivals from the old building in Creechurch Lane; the reason why the others are so uncomfortable is said to be that Avis was a Puritan.

In the 19th century the synagogue was almost closed, as the long-established Jewish community had moved out of the City, and poor Jewish immigrants were living further east. Today, services are held early in the morning on weekdays for employees of the surrounding banks. Judaism has been practised in Bevis Marks Synagogue without interruption for over 300 years, making it unique in all of Europe.

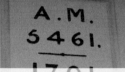

Address Bevis Marks, E1 7AA | Transport Aldgate (Central, Metropolitan Line) | Opening times Mon, Wed, Thu 10.30am–2pm, Tue and Fri 10.30am–1pm, Sun 10.30am–12.30pm | The Jewish Museum in Camden (129 Albert St, Tube to Camden Town, Sun–Thu 10am–5pm, Fri 10am–2pm) presents Jewish culture and the history of Judaism in Britain.

10_ Borough Market
Heaven for foodies

Records from the 13th century refer to traders who sold fruit and vegetables on the main road now called Borough High Street. This place has always been a major traffic junction where roads converged on London Bridge, and today, in 19th-century cast-iron halls directly beneath a railway viaduct, the market activity is accompanied by the rumbling of carriages and metallic screeching. Southwark has always been the poor relation of the City of London across the river. Despite pockets of prosperity, social problems remain in the area. Borough Market is run as a registered charity, a trust that is obliged to invest profits in local projects, and has thrived in recent years as a place where food-lovers find the ingredients for a good dinner party.

A committee of experts jealously guards the market's reputation for gourmet shopping by checking the quality and origin of the goods. This ensures an invigorating mix of British and foreign foods: cheese from Cheshire and Wensleydale is sold alongside brie and mozzarella, English loaves next to rye bread and pretzels from London's German bakery. Fishmongers sell the fresh catch from their own boats on the south coast. Customers who are tired of beef can buy camel, llama or kangaroo meat, and many of the products were scarcely known a generation ago: apple juice from a single variety of fruit, ice cream from goat's milk, more kinds of mushrooms than most people can name.

It was inevitable that a trendy scene for foodies would spring up in the surrounding streets – a tapas bar and a chocolatier, an oyster bar and a specialist roast-beef restaurant. Good street food is easier on the wallet here, and many like to buy paella or pie from a cooked-food stall and eat it in the garden of Southwark Cathedral. The wares on Borough Market may not be cheap, but the quality is high, and bargains are to be had as closing time approaches.

Address South side of Southwark Cathedral, SE1 9DA | **Transport** London Bridge (Jubilee, Northern Line) | **Opening times** Wed–Thu 10am–5pm, Fri 10am–6pm, Sat 8am–5pm | **Tip** The George Inn on Borough High Street, a coaching inn dating from 1676 with a galleried courtyard, is still a cosy pub that serves good ales.

11___The Bottle Kiln in Notting Hill

Slums and piggeries

Bathed in a romantic glow by the film of the same name starring Julia Roberts and Hugh Grant, Notting Hill is regarded as one of the most desirable residential areas in London. This was not always the case. To glimpse humbler origins, walk from Notting Hill Gate Tube station to Walmer Road via Ladbroke Square and Ladbroke Grove, then left into Lansdowne Crescent and along Clarendon Cross and Hippodrome Place. The houses here, with fine stucco façades and beautiful gardens, are coveted by high earners from the City and investors from abroad who see property in London as a safe haven for their money.

The destination is a dark brick structure named a »bottle kiln« on account of its shape, in Walmer Road opposite Avondale Park. It survives from the early 19th century, when the heavy clay found here was fired to make bricks and tiles. This was one of London's most dangerous and insalubrious areas, as the brick workers were an extremely rough bunch and pig-keeping turned the clay pits into evil-smelling pools – the largest of which, »the ocean«, was made into Avondale Park in 1892.

In 1837 a race course, the Hippodrome, opened on the hill, but the stench, slums and undesirable neighbours condemned it to failure. From 1840 the landowners, the Ladbroke family, developed Notting Hill as a fashionable place to live. However, poverty returned in the 20th century, when the large houses were subdivided into flats, and Notting Hill was known for race riots and exploitative landlords. Tentative gentrification started in the 1970s, when decaying houses could be bought for a few thousand pounds. They are worth millions now. The façades have been repaired and painted – but behind the stucco, after all the ups and downs, remain bricks made from London clay.

Address Walmer Road, W11 4LR | Transport Notting Hill Gate (Central, Circle, District Line) | Tip In The Windsor Castle (114 Campden Hill Road), a historic pub dating from 1826, down-to-earth food, ale and cider are served.

12 Brompton Cemetery

Morbid splendour

Death seemed to present a promising financial opportunity when Brompton Cemetery opened in 1840. With 2.5 million inhabitants, London was the world's most populous city. Its ancient graveyards were over-filled, so Parliament approved the founding of seven commercial necropolises. The West of London and Westminster Cemetery Company decided to make imposing architecture its selling point, and laid out a 600-metre-long avenue of limes leading from the north gate to elevated colonnades, extensive catacombs and a domed octagonal chapel. The protests of small shareholders prevented further extravagance, but the company had over-reached itself and was forced to sell out after twelve years of operation. The purchaser, the government, had picked up a bargain, as the burial business began to flourish.

The round lawn between the colonnades, intended as an open space, was soon covered with graves when Queen Victoria's servant Julius Kanné was laid to rest there. Today the pomp and pathos of Victorian days – decorated Celtic crosses and mourning angels, plain upright stones and marble mausoleums with metal doors – share the cemetery with burgeoning nature, as the 20th century spurned ostentatious forms of burial. Many graves were neglected, leaving Brompton Cemetery in a state of picturesque deterioration. Weathered stones lie in deep shade. Grasses grow tall to the left and right of the central avenue, moss fills the hollows of inscriptions, ferns and brambles grow unchecked. The 16-hectare site is a biotope harbouring several families of foxes, 200 species of moths and butterflies, a great variety of birds and countless wild flowers, undisturbed by traffic and visited by few.

Those who appreciate overgrown, morbid decay should avoid the south-west corner of the cemetery, where the stands of the Chelsea football ground, bright and ugly, tower above graves and bushes.

Address Between Old Brompton Road and Fulham Road, SW10 9UG | Transport West Brompton (District Line) | Opening times Daily from 8am, May–Aug until 8pm; March, Sept until 6pm; Feb, Oct until 5pm; Nov–Jan until 4pm. Tours May–Aug Sun 2pm from South Lodge, Fulham Road. | Tip For a violent contrast to the cemetery, visit Chelsea Football Club's stadium and museum (entrance by the west stand in Fulham Road, tours daily every 30 minutes from 10am to 3pm).

13___The Brunswick Plane

The urban tree

London's characteristic tree is the plane. It adorns many streets with broad leaves and bark that varies in colour from grey and brown to green and mauve. It shades office workers during their midday break, nourishes squirrels with its seeds, and after the leaves have fallen, the plane's attractive spherical fruit remains hanging for months more. One of the most magnificent examples of the species, the »Brunswick plane«, stands on the lawn in Brunswick Square. Its circumference measures seven metres. Because, unusually, its lower branches were not cut off, this specimen spreads out at head height. At the centre of a wide expanse of grass, the tree had the freedom to grow in its splendid natural shape.

The London plane (Platanus x acerifolia), is a separate species, probably a cross of the oriental plane (P. orientalis) and the American sycamore (P. occidentalis). In cities it attains a height of 30 to 35 metres, in the country 45 metres or more in exceptional cases. Its suitability as an urban tree was recognised in the 18th century. It is resistant against frost, drought, waterlogged conditions, compacted soil and – most important of all in the days of London smog – against pollution. Toxins cannot easily penetrate the tree, as its bark flakes off in patches and rain washes its hard, shiny leaves. It is not known how long a London plane can live, as none is thought to have died of old age. Some are 350 years old.

The tree on Brunswick Square, which has outlasted the original surrounding buildings, was probably planted between 1795 and 1802, a time when this part of Bloomsbury was a fine address: in Jane Austen's »Emma«, Mr and Mrs Knightley live on Brunswick Square. It is included on the list of »Great Trees of London« along with many other planes, notably the Victorian specimen on Berkeley Square and a famous one by the entrance to the Dorchester Hotel.

Address Brunswick Square, WC1N 1AZ | Transport Russell Square (Piccadilly Line) | Tip For refreshments or culture: the Foundling Museum at the north-east corner of Brunswick Square has an exquisite art collection, including works by Hogarth and Gainsborough, and a good café (Tue–Sat 10am–5pm, Sun 11am–5pm).

14___Bunhill Fields
Lunch among the tombstones

Green spaces are precious in the City. Office workers who cannot face the idea of eating with their colleagues in the canteen yet again, buy a sandwich or a salad and take it to a bench in a nearby park. And if the park happens to be a cemetery, as in the case of Bunhill Fields on the northern edge of the finance district, why should that spoil their appetite?

The name derives from »bone hill«. In the 16th century, human remains were piled up here on marshy ground and covered with earth, as the ossuary of St Paul's Cathedral was full to the brim. After the Great Plague of 1665, thousands more bodies were dumped on the site, which then remained in use as an unconsecrated burial ground – not for Anglicans but for Dissenters, i.e. members of the Baptist, Quaker and other Protestant groups. By the time the cemetery was closed in 1852, tens of thousands had been laid to rest here, including some prominent persons: Daniel Defoe, the author of »Robinson Crusoe«; the itinerant preacher John Bunyan, who wrote »The Pilgrim's Progress«; and the visionary poet and artist William Blake.

In the 19th century, and again in the 1960s following war damage, Bunhill Fields was made into a park. Mossy stones, crosses leaning at an angle and a few massive, ivy-covered tombs stand in densely packed rows beneath plane, oak, ash and sycamore trees. Defoe is honoured by an obelisk, Bunyan by a large tomb bearing the image of a pilgrim. Perhaps the most edifying grave of all is that of Mary Page, with an inscription detailing the sufferings that she endured with Christian fortitude: she had so much fluid in her body that it had to be tapped 66 times in the space of 67 months, extracting no less than 240 gallons altogether. Relaxing on seats with a view of this medical history, office workers from the City wash down their ciabatta and baguette with gallons of caffè latte.

Address Between City Road and Bunhill Row, EC1Y 2BG | Transport Old Street (Northern Line) | Opening times April–Sept Mon–Fri 7.30am–7pm, Sat, Sun 9.30am–7pm; Oct–March Mon–Fri 7.30am–4pm, Sat, Sun 9.30am–4pm | Tip Directly opposite Bunhill Fields on City Road are the chapel and house of John Wesley (1703–91), the founder of Methodism. A museum there is devoted to the history of this denomination (Mon–Sat 10am–4pm).

15_ Cabbies' Shelter in Grosvenor Gardens

Huts that are architectural heritage

London taxis are famous around the world, of course. Some 21,000 »black cabs« – the name sticks despite their modern appearance in all sorts of garish colours – operate on the city's streets. Less well known and much less numerous are the green-painted wooden huts that were built in the late 19th century as places of rest and refreshment for the drivers of hansom cabs. 13 of them are still standing, every one a listed structure and thus protected from demolition. 150 years ago, the drivers of two-wheeled hansom cabs were not allowed to leave their vehicles during a shift, and therefore seldom got a warm meal although they were out in all weathers. A charity called the Cabmen's Shelter Fund took pity on them and built 61 huts at cab ranks between 1875 and 1914. As they stood on public highways, the shelters were not allowed to occupy a surface larger than a horse and carriage, but each of them was fitted with a small kitchen and seating for ten to twelve persons. Alcohol and gambling were banned – the approved pastime was to read improving literature donated by publishers.

Some cabbies' shelters, like that in Grosvenor Gardens and those on Hanover Square, next to Temple Tube station and in Thurloe Place opposite the Victoria and Albert Museum, still serve tea, coffee, sandwiches and light meals to taxi drivers. Others, such as the huts on Russell Square and near Embankment station, are deserted, no more than lifeless monuments to days that have passed. Despite the modest size of the shelters, they have architectural dignity thanks to a harmonious composition of windows, panels and perforated decoration in the shape of plant motifs. Small triangles like pediments provide ventilation, a chimney surmounts the roof of wooden shingles, and overhanging eaves protect customers when they buy their tea. It is a simple and attractive design.

The chalkboard menu reads:

Breakfast sticks
Hot Dogs
Burger + chips
Hot MEAT Sticks
Jacket Potatoes

Address Grosvenor Gardens, west side, SW1W | **Transport** Victoria (Circle, District, Victoria Line) | **Tip** In the Royal Mews at Buckingham Palace, the Queen's collection of limousines is on display (April–Oct Mon–Sat 10am–5pm; Nov, Feb, March Mon–Sat 10am–4pm; Dec–Jan closed). Unfortunately, it does not include the private taxi that Prince Philip uses to get about town without attracting attention.

16__ Café E. Pellicci

A piece of the old East End

Things ain't what they used to be: Shoreditch and Spitalfields, once down-at-heel, are buzzing with artists and fashion designers. But a lot will have to change before Bethnal Green Road becomes hip. Along this shabby street, Bangladeshi immigrants have added another layer to the old East End. The stalls of the street market are laden with cabbages and Asian fruits, plastic buckets and brand-name cosmetics at rock-bottom prices. The shop windows behind them display brightly coloured saris, discounted furniture, shisha pipes and prayer rugs. On one side of the road stands a church, on the other a halal take-away.

In the middle of all this, a living relic of a past generation shows that immigration is nothing new. Around 1900, when many farm labourers from Italy came to this area, a couple named Pellicci started a café. Their son Nevio was born in the flat above it and, with his wife from the home village in Tuscany, ran the café until his death in 2008. The Pelliccis learned to speak English like their neighbours and cook what the locals wanted to eat. Today, Nevio junior carries on the same way and greets regular customers by name, as his father once welcomed the Kray twins. Bacon & eggs feature on the menu alongside lasagne. Photos of Pellicci ancestors line the walls. The façade of yellow Vitrolite and steel and the wonderful wooden marquetry interior, the work of an Italian carpenter in 1946, are unchanged. Declaring it »an … increasingly rare example of the intact and stylish Italian café that flourished in London in the inter-war years«, English Heritage listed the café.

One thing that no conservationist can officially protect is the atmosphere: noisy banter, orders shouted through from the counter to the back kitchen, and the mingled steam and aromas emanating from the Espresso machine, malt vinegar on chips, and ketchup on sausage. Perhaps things are what they used to be.

Address 332 Bethnal Green Road, E2 0AG | Transport Bethnal Green (Central Line) | Opening times Mon–Sat 7am–4pm | Tip One more bright thread in the multicultural tapestry of Bethnal Green is the London Buddhist Centre (51 Roman Road), which holds courses on meditation and Buddhism and runs a bookshop (Mon–Sat 10am–5pm, www.lbc.org.uk).

17__Centre Point

Extremely coarse or worth preserving?

The high-rises of the City huddle together in groups. In the West End, by contrast, one solitary tower soars boldly above its surroundings. Centre Point, London's tallest building when it was completed in 1963, resulted from the collaboration of two controversial men. The property developer Harry Hyams chose as his architect Richard Seifert, whose skill in negotiating with the authorities gained permission for a skyscraper with an unprecedented height of 117 metres and a 150-year lease at a fixed sum. In return, the unbuilt part of the site was to be made available to traffic.

Hyams made his fortune by letting large properties to a single customer rather than many small tenants. For the 20,000 square metres of Centre Point, which was widely held to be a monstrosity, he found no taker and left the whole tower empty, judging the prospect of a high rent at some future date to be a better option than a low rent for the duration of the usual long-term contract.

This state of affairs continued for 15 years and was seen as a scandal at a time of housing shortages, even though Centre Point was not a residential building. Squatters moved in and were evicted again. The local authority threatened compulsory purchase, and wild rumours circulated: the government was subsidising a predatory capitalist, it was said, because it wanted to use the tower and the Tube station beneath in the event of nuclear war.

As for the architect, Seifert put his stamp on London's skyline in the 1960s and 1970s as no-one had done since Christopher Wren 300 years earlier. The architectural historian Nikolaus Pevsner described Centre Point as »extremely coarse«, but as time passed its slender, convex outline and Y-shaped window elements found favour, was even compared with Wren's church steeples, and is now a listed building.

In 2015, work began to convert it into 82 luxury residences.

Address 101 New Oxford Street, WC1A 1DD | **Transport** Tottenham Court Road (Central, Northern Line) | **Tip** The café on the top floor of Foyles bookshop (107 Charing Cross Road) is a great place to take a break in this area.

18_Chalybeate Well
Hampstead's healing water

The fountain in Well Walk that a charitable lady named Susanna Knowle donated to the poor of Hampstead in December 1698 is dry and neglected. Below her coat of arms, an inscription declares that this is the »Chalybeate Well«, a name that refers to the iron content of its water. In Greek mythology, the first use of iron tools was ascribed to a people called the Chalybes.

Poor people are not much in evidence today in this leafy suburb, which offers respite from central London for the wealthy. Hampstead's prosperity began in the same way 350 years ago, when it was a village of 600 residents. During the plague year of 1665, many Londoners sought refuge here, as the air and water were good. They escaped to higher ground from the stink and filth of narrow streets, preferring the vistas and the fresh breezes up on Hampstead Heath. At about the same time, the supposedly healing properties of the local springs were discovered. A local physician, Doctor Gibbon, praised the efficacy of the water against intestinal worms, hysteria and excessive moisture in the brain. In the 18th century, Hampstead was a flourishing spa, where polite society took the waters in the Pump Room and danced in the Long Room. Water was taken from a spring in Well Road (parallel to Well Walk) and bottled on the site where The Flask tavern now stands.

As the spa was no longer fashionable in the 19th century, its buildings opposite the Chalybeate Well were demolished in 1882. Although the waters no longer flowed, the climate was still healthy. Mount Vernon Hospital was built on an elevation further north to heal diseases of the lungs. Its imposing Victorian edifice was converted to apartments for celebrities, as singers and actors appreciate good air. Down the hill in Hampstead village, only an unused fountain and street names like Well Walk preserve the memory of Hampstead's days as a spa.

Address Well Walk, NW3 1BX | **Transport** Hampstead (Northern Line) | **Tip** Burgh House, once the residence of Dr Gibbon, houses an exhibition on the history of Hampstead and the charming Buttery Café with tables in the garden (New End Square, turn right at the lower end of Well Walk; Wed–Fri 11am–5pm, Sat and Sun 9.30am–5pm

19___Cheyne Walk
Mixed company

Has any street in England been home to so many famous residents? Its attractions are obvious: until the 19th century, Cheyne Walk lay right on the banks of the Thames. Today, well-tended gardens screen it from the thundering traffic of Chelsea Embankment.

One of the first notables to discover the charms of Chelsea was Sir Thomas More, saint, scholar and Lord Chancellor to Henry VIII. From his estate to the west of Cheyne Walk, More could reach Westminster by boat to attend on his king. Although Henry had More beheaded in 1535, the king followed his adviser's example a year later, buying a country house on the site that is now nos. 19 to 26, Cheyne Walk. Two of his wives, Catherine Parr and Anne of Cleves, as well as his daughter, the future Queen Elizabeth I, spent time here. Later the house belonged to Sir Hans Sloane, whose scientific collections formed the basis of the British Museum.

Most of the houses in Cheyne Walk date from the early 18th century. Many are sheltered behind creeper-covered walls and fine wrought-iron gates, but passers-by can glimpse rose gardens, columned entrances and Regency-style balconies with curved roofs. The roll-call of occupants is astonishing: Rolling Stone Keith Richards lived at no. 3, Mick Jagger and Marianne Faithfull spent a short time at no. 48 in 1968, and no. 13 was home to the composer Ralph Vaughan Williams. Artists also liked the spot: Dante Gabriel Rossetti lived at no. 16, James McNeill Whistler at no. 21, and J. M. W. Turner died at no. 119. Literature is represented by George Eliot (no. 4), the poet Swinburne (no. 16 again) and Henry James (no. 21). Not to forget a prime minister (David Lloyd George at no. 10), the great engineers Marc and Isambard Kingdom Brunel (number 98), the footballer George Best, and John Paul Getty II. And around the corner on Oakley Street, Bob Marley wrote »I Shot the Sheriff«.

Address Cheyne Walk, SW3 5LR | Transport Sloane Square (District, Circle Line);
bus no. 170 from Victoria Station to Albert Bridge | Tip Chelsea Physic Garden at the
eastern end of Cheyne Walk (April–Oct Tue–Fri and Sun 11am–6pm) was founded in
1673 to cultivate medicinal herbs. Lunch and afternoon tea are served in its café.

20__Chinatown

An enclave in Soho

Immigrant communities have put their stamp on a number of different districts in London. These are usually poor areas outside the city centre. South Lambeth Road is Little Portugal, Edgware Road has a marked Arab character, and way out west, Southall has a large Punjabi population. Thanks to its location in the West End, Chinatown is different. A small area around Gerrard Street and Lisle Street is home to 80 Chinese restaurants. Red-painted Chinese arches with green-glazed roof tiles greet crowds of visitors, two pop-eyed stone lions glower up Macclesfield Street, crispy brown Peking duck hangs in the windows, and streets are named in Chinese characters. Chinatown is a colourful, bustling tourist attraction – but is it authentic?

In the 18th century, sailors from the Far East lived in dockland areas such as Limehouse, which was known for its Chinese laundries 100 years ago. Bombing in the Second World War scattered this community, but a regrouping took place after the war thanks to the return of British soldiers. Some of them had acquired a taste for Asian food. The first Chinese restaurants opened in seedy Soho, where rents were low. As Cantonese immigrants arrived from Hong Kong, the area slowly acquired its character, which is more than a row of eateries for visitors. Chinese really do live here, working in supermarkets, bakeries, herbalists and medicinal practices as well as restaurants. They have their own lawyers, travel agents and accountants. In Charing Cross Road, the Westminster Chinese Library was established, in Leicester Court the Chinese Community Centre.

Paradoxically, apart from this single high concentration around Gerrard Street, London's estimated 100,000 residents of Chinese origin are thinly spread across the city. The reason may be that many of them still run restaurants, which prosper in the suburbs by keeping a distance from their rivals.

Address Between Shaftesbury Avenue and Leicester Square, W1D 5PJ | Transport Leicester Square (Northern, Piccadilly Line) | Tip Vietnamese restaurants can be found on Kingsland Road in Shoreditch (bus no. 149 or 242 from Liverpool Street Station).

21 Christie's

Classier than eBay

London's art scene comprises world-class museums with famous paintings and cutting-edge East End galleries, famous artists and anonymous but talented sprayers. Three long-established auction houses belong to the conventional end of this spectrum: Sotheby's in Bond Street, Bonham's in New Bond Street – and Christie's, founded in 1760 and domiciled in King Street in the St James's district since 1823.

Is the National Gallery too crowded, and the latest special exhibition at the British Museum too expensive? For a quieter alternative that is free of charge, it is worth paying a visit to an auction house where paintings, exquisite furniture, sculptures, objets d'art and everything else that rich collectors covet are on display. The viewing dates can be seen on the auction houses' internet sites. Anyone can walk in and look around. Discreet, polite, well-informed members of staff may approach with advice or information, but no-one need fear being put under pressure or made to feel embarrassed about their ignorance. Most people, however, will be more at ease if they are well-dressed when they enter the well-appointed premises. So don't be shy, just walk inside and ascend the stairs that lead to three museum-like galleries. Beyond them lies the auction room with its rows of seats and auctioneer's desk.

Christie's employs experts for every imaginable field: old masters and contemporary painting, art from Africa and Oceania, jewellery, silver, carpets, cigars and wine. Trustworthy guests may pick up or touch items that would be locked behind glass in the Victoria and Albert Museum. If the exhibits do not appeal, it is entertaining to watch the other visitors: distinguished older men, elegant ladies, girls in jeans who seem to be in their teens but might be billionaires' daughters. Which of them will be bidding in the auction tomorrow?

Address 8 King Street, SW1Y 6QT | **Transport** Green Park (Jubilee, Piccadilly, Victoria Line) | **Opening times** Mon–Fri 9.30am–4.30pm, www.christies.com | **Tip** The branch of Christie's at 85 Old Brompton Road, South Kensington, is livelier. Antiques, the contents of whole houses, music and sports memorabilia and much more are auctioned here.

22_ City Hall
A skewed seat of government

What a location! City Hall lies on the south bank of the Thames next to Tower Bridge, with a fine view across the river to the Tower of London and the skyscrapers of the financial district. On a site like this, when building a new seat of government for one of the world's greatest cities, architecture of high calibre was called for. The result, a ten-storey modified sphere with a pronounced lean, met with acclaim from some quarters, but has also been described as a misshapen egg, Darth Vader's helmet, and a glass testicle.

Why did London get a new City Hall in 2002? Opposite it on the north bank is the historic City of London, the »square mile«, now mainly a banking district. This precinct has its own ancient seat of government, Guildhall, and a lord mayor with ceremonial duties. City Hall by contrast is the headquarters of the Greater London Authority, which administers the whole metropolitan area. It is run by the Mayor of London and London Assembly. Because the left-wing Greater London Council was a thorn in Margaret Thatcher's flesh in the 1980s, she dissolved it. The city had separate councils for various regions, but no overall administration until the Labour government restored it and instituted the first directly elected mayor for all of London in 2000.

This called for a new seat of government, City Hall, designed by the renowned architects Foster and Partners. They used a lot of glass to symbolise open government. A 500-metre spiral ramp from the basement to the top floor surrounds the assembly chamber and affords views inside, making speakers feel like goldfish in a giant bowl. The most striking aspect of the building, its 31-degree southward tilt, makes it energy-efficient. On the lower storey, where the floor covering is a satellite image of London, the café is open to everybody. City Hall is like a metaphor for London itself: surprising, provocative, lovably out of kilter.

Address The Queen's Walk, SE12AA | Transport London Bridge (Jubilee, Northern Line) | Opening times Mon–Thu 8.30am–6pm, Fri 8.30am–5.30pm | Tip A few minutes' walk west along the river bank is Hay's Galleria, a warehouse with wharf that has been converted to an atrium of restaurants and shops.

23__The Coade Stone Lion
Unexpectedly humble origins

The eastern approach to Westminster Bridge is guarded by a majestic stone lion with a luxuriant mane. From its granite plinth on the north parapet of the bridge, it watches over those who cross the Thames towards Parliament. It might be thought a worthy symbol of power from the days when London was the capital of a global empire – but in fact this is a brewery lion, and is not even made of real stone.

The material is »Coade stone«, a ceramic product that was made in the factory of Mrs Eleanor Coade in Lambeth between 1770 and the 1840s. The recipe was 60 per cent clay with additions of ground glass, flint and a little quartz. Coade stone was extremely resistant to weathering and corrosion caused by soot, important properties in smoggy 19th-century London. The mixture was shaped in moulds to make unique items or low-cost mass products, and was fired four days long at a high, constant temperature. This technical achievement, and the fact that standard parts could be combined in varied ways for individual designs, made Coade stone popular for monuments and architectural adornment. Further examples of its use are the figures above the entrance of Twinings on The Strand (see p. 208), the tombs of the Sealy family and Captain Bligh (of the mutiny on the *Bounty*) in the churchyard of St Mary's Lambeth (see p. 224), and architectural details in the chapel of the Old Naval College in Greenwich.

In 1837, the sculptor William Woodington made two lions to stand on top of the Red Lion Brewery on the south bank of the Thames. When the brewery was demolished in 1950 and the Festival of Britain was held on its site, the red paint was stripped from one lion and, at the wish of King George VI, the figure was placed in front of Waterloo Station. It came to the bridge in 1966. The second lion, shining gold, growls down at visitors from the gate of Twickenham rugby stadium.

Address Westminster Bridge Road, SE1 7PB | Transport Westminster (Circle, District, Jubilee Line) | Tip One legacy of the Festival of Britain is an example of good 1950s architecture: the Royal Festival Hall, with the upmarket bar-restaurant Skylon and a view of the river from the café.

24__College Garden

A hidden monastic garden

A tourist and his money are soon parted, as the throng around West-minster Abbey demonstrates. »Queue here to pay by credit card«, proclaim the signs, but the steep admission price does not seem to keep the crowds away. The atmosphere is calmer in College Garden, directly to the south of the church, and it costs nothing to get in. If you stand in front of the abbey with the towers straight ahead, a gate on the right leads to Dean's Yard, a large open space with a lawn at the centre. After passing through, look out on the left for a smaller entrance with a pointed arch and a metal gate. The dark passage be-yond it leads past the Great Cloister to the Little Cloister with its fountain, then to the garden on the right.

College Garden has probably been tended without interruption for 900 years, which makes it the oldest in England in continuous use. In the Middle Ages, Benedictine monks cultivated herbs for medicine and the kitchen here. They also had vegetable patches to grow onions, beans and cabbages, fish ponds, beehives and an or-chard, whose products were shared with the local poor on the feast of St James. Part of the plot was a flower garden. After the dissolu-tion of the monastery in 1540, Westminster Abbey became a colle-giate church under the direct jurisdiction of the monarch, and the gardening work carried on as before.

Vegetables, an herb garden, and fruit trees bearing apples, quinces and mulberries uphold the monastic tradition. The plane trees on the lawn were planted in 1850. There is a splashing fountain and a fragrant rose garden. The classical building to the west belongs to Westminster School, which was founded in 1560 by Elizabeth I but originated in a monks' school back in the 12th century. Out in Dean's Yard, the pupils can sometimes be seen playing a noisy game of football, but the secluded College Garden remains a peaceful spot.

Address Dean's Yard, SW1P 3PF | Transport Westminster (Circle, District, Jubilee Line) |
Opening times Check on www.westminster-abbey.org | Tip For a view of Parliament and
the Thames without crowds, go to Victoria Tower Garden on Abingdon Street. A monument
to the campaigner for women's rights Emmeline Pankhurst and a cast of Rodin's sculpture
»The Burghers of Calais« can be seen here.

25__Cousin Lane Stairs

Down to a beach on the Thames

In centuries past, when rowing boats carried passengers along the river, many flights of steps were needed to give access to landing stages. In the heart of the city, few such stairs have survived, one of them at the end of Cousin Lane. Here you can descend to a hidden beach at ebb tide (but take care, as the steps can be slippery), in order to see, hear and smell London from an unfamiliar angle.

Down on the shore, the noise of road traffic recedes, but trains rumble across Cannon Street Bridge, and the waves from Thames Clippers splash up on the little beach. Pebbles crunch beneath your feet. Looking down, you see stones of many colours, pieces of brick rounded by the river current, shards of pottery, animal bones and oyster shells, and at low water, you can walk across this uneven ground for about 100 metres in both directions for a water-snail's view of bridges and embankments.

This is not the prosperous, shiny surface of London, but its many-layered underside. The high quayside walls, full of holes and patched up in brick, are covered in green slime and fronds. Heavy chains hang from them, and rotting timbers rise from the river bed. A round iron gate in the wall and a concrete channel for its outflow are reminders of the dank warren of sewers and underground streams that lies beneath the streets. The Walbrook, which flowed through the Roman and medieval city, reached the Thames close to this spot. On beaches like this, the tides and river current scour the river bed and bring London's past to light. In the late 1950s, a 14th-century sword was turned up close by. Broken clay pipes and coins are found all the time by Thames mudlarks, whose hobby is digging up history in the Thames.

The atmosphere of Cousin Lane Stairs has been captured by a wonderful project, www.soundsurvey.org.uk, which presents an acoustic map by means of recordings made all over the city.

Address Between Thames Street and the river, immediately west of Cannon Street Station, EC4R 3TE | **Transport** Cannon Street (Circle, District Line). | **Tip** Next to Cousin Lane Stairs, the dark, uninviting Steelyard Passage leads beneath the railway bridge. From the 13th century, the Steelyard was the London depot of the Hanseatic League of German trading cities. A plaque on the east side of the bridge commemorates it.

26__Cross Bones Graveyard

In memory of the outcast and downtrodden

A patch of wasteland behind a high wall in a run-down corner of Southwark has become a shrine and a place of popular protest. Passers-by can see little through the locked metal gates, as they are covered from top to bottom with colourful strips of cloth, plastic flowers, scraps of paper inscribed with prayers, poems, and hand-written messages to deceased relatives, Christmas tree decorations, teddy bears and crocheted dolls, dream catchers, images of Indian goddesses, small mirrors, chestnuts threaded on string. Many people have expressed their wishes and emotions here through words and objects. A Madonna hangs from the gate, but this is no Christian sanctuary – in fact, it was an unconsecrated graveyard.

Until the 17th century, prostitutes, known as »Winchester geese«, were buried here within the jurisdiction of the bishops of Winchester. Beyond the control of the City of London authorities, the see of Winchester licensed brothels, arenas for bull baiting, and theatres. The bishops profited from this business, but gave no Christian burial to »dishonoured« women. Crossbones later became a Christian cemetery for the poor and was closed in 1852, when an estimated 15,000 graves had filled it to overflowing. In the 1990s, archaeologists who examined 148 skeletons from the site found one third of them to be new-born or still-born children.

Although this unbuilt site is a mouth-watering prospect for developers, all schemes have so far been prevented by residents and an alliance including mystics, feminists and the local writer John Constable, whose »Southwark Mysteries« were inspired, he claims, by the spirit of a Winchester goose. Since 1998, ceremonies have been held here at Halloween. The campaign for the graveyard to be made into a memorial park for »the outcast dead« has persuaded the landowner, Transport for London, to lease the site to the Bankside Open Spaces Trust, which is raising money to create a garden.

OCTOBER

2004
23rd June.
the first Cross

ELIZABETH

is place of he
ll remember a
yers for the m
women of Brad
honour them as
FOR ALL THAT T
AND COULD HA
R.I.P.
uesn

RGE HU

gil hel

Address Redcross Way, SE1 1TA | Transport Borough (Northern Line) | Tip On the Thames path close to Southwark Cathedral stands a high wall with a rose window – remains of the magnificent palace of the bishops of Winchester, which stood here from the 12th to the 17th century.

27 __ Dr Johnson's House

A dictionary and a cat

Hodge was »a very fine cat indeed«, said Dr Samuel Johnson (1709–84) to his biographer James Boswell. In keeping with this praise, the monument on Gough Square shows not the great man of letters himself but the cat, sitting on its master's dictionary next to a couple of oyster shells. Johnson personally bought the oysters, as his servants would have found it insulting to be sent to buy food for an animal, and Hodge would doubtless have been made to suffer.

Johnson's solid-looking house of red brick with large windows stands at the opposite end of the small square. Despite its sparse furnishings, the wood-panelled interior conveys a good impression of an 18th-century dwelling. Portraits of his friends, including one of Johnson's biographer James Boswell, hang on the walls. Like other writers struggling to make ends meet, Johnson lived under the shadow of a possible visit by the bailiff or a spell in a debtors' prison. This explains the spyhole next to the front door and the stout chain placed over an iron upright – its corkscrew form designed to prevent anyone from hooking off the chain through the window. The metal bars in the fanlight were meant to stop children climbing in and opening up to burglars.

A brilliant conversationalist at the centre of a learned circle of friends, Johnson was also generous and humane. He paid for the education of his black servant, who was his principal heir, and accommodated a strange group of misfits and losers, from whose pleas and quarrels he escaped to the study at the top of the house. Here he completed single-handedly what was to be the standard dictionary of the English language for 100 years. A team of six clerks who worked standing at a long desk merely helped to copy out the definitions and quotes in a clear hand. The work contains 42,773 words, their meanings explained with the help of 114,000 quotes from a myriad of authors. The most famous entry reads »Lexicographer: a writer of dictionaries, a harmless drudge«.

Address Gough Square 17, EC4A 3DE | **Transport** Blackfriars (Circle, District Line) | **Opening times** Mon–Sat 11am–5pm, May–Sept until 5.30pm | **Tip** The house of the architect Sir John Soane (1753–1837) is an eccentric museum crammed full of art, furniture, ancient Egyptian treasures, personal mementoes – and two mummified cats (13 Lincoln's Inn Fields, Tue–Sat 10am–5pm).

28__ The Duke of York Column
A man who made it to the top

The famous column is of course the one dedicated to Horatio Nelson on Trafalgar Square, but the admiral does not stand as high as a much less glorious contemporary: Frederick, Duke of York. The second son of King George III, his early life was nothing unusual for a prince of German lineage. In 1764, at the age of six months, he was made Prince Bishop of Osnabrück. He later married a daughter of Frederick William II of Prussia.

So far, so good – but then he embarked on a military career, commanding British forces in Flanders against the French revolutionary armies in 1793. After initial successes, he retreated to Hanover, the historic family seat, and sailed home in 1795 without having accomplished much. His father rewarded these exploits by making the Duke of York a field marshal and commander-in-chief of the army. In 1799 his expedition to the Netherlands was so calamitous that he was forced to withdraw after three months. The campaign gave rise to the children's rhyme: »The Grand Old Duke of York, he had ten thousand men, he marched them up to the top of the hill and he marched them down again.«

Back in England, things scarcely improved. His mistress felt obliged to cover household expenses by selling officers' patents, as her royal lover had squandered huge sums on horses. The ensuing scandal forced the Duke to resign his command. He has nevertheless earned praise from army historians for his reforms, which are held to have paved the way for later military successes. After his death in 1827, one day's wages was withheld from every British soldier in order to finance the monument. The Duke of York looks down on St James's Park from a 42-metre granite column. The viewing platform, once a favourite place for suicide, is no longer open to the public. The statue is said to have been placed so high in order to keep the Duke out of reach of his creditors.

Address Waterloo Place, SW1Y 5AH | Transport Charing Cross (Bakerloo, Northern Line) | Tip The café on the lower floor of the National Gallery on Trafalgar Square serves light meals and tempting cakes, the adjacent restaurant finer food in stylish surroundings.

29__Eccleston Mews

Ideal homes in the stables

A »mews«, a small service road at the back of the fine houses of the rich for stables, deliveries and servants, is a London phenomenon. They are common in districts such as Kensington, Mayfair and Bayswater, and almost unknown outside London. Eccleston Mews, built in the 19th century in Belgravia, is one example of many quiet enclaves that can be seen on a walk around London.

When residences for high society with imposing classical architecture were built in terraces around the broad streets and garden squares of Belgravia, it was out of the question that stables or tradesmen's entrances would spoil the view of the façade. The solution was to place a humble street at the back, sometimes semi-concealed behind an archway. Here horses and carriages were accommodated on the ground floor of plain buildings, while grooms and servants could live on the upper floor. In the 20th century, the motor car made these stables obsolete, and ever fewer families could afford a mansion with a large staff of servants. Little by little, mews buildings were converted to garages or dwellings. From the 1950s they came into vogue as affordable, discreet addresses in top locations for creative people. The painter Francis Bacon was among the first artists to inhabit a mews. In the Swinging Sixties, to live in a mews was considered unconventional and slightly racy. In the film »A Hard Day's Night«, the Beatles occupied a mews flat, as did John Steed, the hero of the TV series »The Avengers«.

Apart from the Royal Mews at Buckingham Palace, only one has remained in uninterrupted operation as a stable: Bathurst Mews to the north of Hyde Park is still home to a riding school. Mews houses, enlarged by cellar and attic conversions, are now sold at dizzying prices. Often a Bentley or Jaguar is parked outside, but the street name reveals that these were once homes for horses and servants.

Address Between Eaton Square and Eaton Place, SW1W 9AD | **Transport** Victoria (Circle, District, Victoria Line) | **Tip** William Curley, chocolatier and maker of exquisite ice cream, has a parlour at 198 Ebury Street (Mon–Fri 10am–6.30pm, Sat 9am–7pm, Sun 10am–6pm).

30 — Edgware Road
»Little Beirut« in London

London, where a third of the population was born abroad, is probably more multicultural than any city in the world apart from New York. The faces, clothing and languages spoken make it obvious that dozens of different ethnic groups live here. Some concentrate in a particular area – east Africans in North Kensington, for example, Turks in Dalston. European and English-speaking immigrants also have their favourite quarters. Five per cent of the residents in Chelsea are US citizens, and a Cypriot community has congregated in Camberwell. Lovers of Portuguese food head for South Lambeth Road, and those who like Arab cooking are spoiled for choice on Edgware Road.

At its southern end near Marble Arch, expensive Lebanese restaurants put on live music and belly-dancing. Further out, north of Edgware Road Tube station, a simpler style takes over. Syrians and Iraqis run grocery stores and eateries with plain furnishings that serve delicious meals for a low price. Newsagents sell Arabic newspapers, fashion outlets cater for ladies who prefer to reveal little, and numerous TV screens show the latest football match from Egypt or the news from Al Jazeera channel. When the weather is fine, cafés in Praed Street put shisha pipes out on the pavement.

Arabs trading with the Ottoman Empire settled in this area 100 years ago. In the 1950s, many Egyptians arrived, and since then every crisis in the Middle East has brought more immigrants. Lebanese, Iraqis and Palestinians fled from war, Algerians from violent civil unrest, Syrians from political persecution. While rich Arabs in search of sound investments and desirable residences have bought property in Knightsbridge – although the Egyptian Mohamed al-Fayed no longer owns Harrods – and Mayfair, to enjoy some Arab atmosphere, avoid these haunts of the super-rich and walk across Hyde Park to Edgware Road.

Address Edgware Road, W2 2HZ: walk north-west from Marble Arch | Transport
Edgware Road (Circle, District Line) | Tip The Subway Gallery (in the pedestrian subway
at the crossing of Edgware Rd. and Harrow Rd., Mon–Sat 11am–7pm) presents changing
exhibitions of Underground Art with a tendency to the provocative.

31__Eel Pie Island
A refuge for artists and musicians

This island in the Thames takes its name from the fare that was served in inns in the 18th and 19th centuries, when guests came by boat for dances. Today, a narrow pedestrian bridge leads to tranquillity and seclusion in leafy surroundings rather than pies and dance music. There are no cars on the island, not even bicycles – just a path leading to Richmond Yacht Club, Twickenham Rowing Club and 50 houses, whose occupants clearly value their peace and quiet, as signs politely point out that the gardens are private property. On two weekends in summer, when 20 or more artists, including painters, sculptors, potters and glass artists, open their studios, visitors are allowed to see more. In a yard on the north bank, ship's carpenters, welders and metalworkers repair and build boats. Sedate cabin cruisers and sleek motor yachts bob up and down by the quay and in boathouses. The two tips of the 700-metre-long island are nature reserves.

The island has not always been a mix of residential idyll and place of work. In the 1950s, the run-down Eel Pie Hotel, known in the pre-war years for its genteel tea dances, was a venue for hot new music and one of the best places for British jazz.

Rhythm 'n' blues and rock were the thing in the early 60s. Rod Stewart, The Who, Pink Floyd and The Rolling Stones all played on Eel Pie Island before they became famous. The activities of the bands and their fans made the island notorious. Alerted by its aura of sex and drugs, the local authority demanded expensive improvements to the hotel. It was forced to close in 1967, a group of anarchists moved in, and soon the building was home to the largest hippie commune in England. The party was short-lived: the hotel burned to the ground in 1971, cause unknown. More than 40 years on, artists lend a little glamour to Eel Pie Island, but it no longer has a dubious reputation.

Address In Twickenham, West London, TW1 3DY | **Transport** Twickenham (Overground), then 10 minutes' walk; bus R 68 from Richmond to King Street. To see the island without setting foot on it, take a boat trip from Richmond: June – Sept daily; April, May at weekends. | **Tip** The White Swan on the north bank of the Thames opposite the eastern tip of Eel Pie Island is a 300-year-old pub with lots of charm and good food (daily 11am – 10.30pm).

32 Electric Avenue
Reggae or salsa, dreadlocks or a wig?

In the 1880s, a new shopping street in then-prosperous Brixton was a wonder to behold: it had electric lighting, which provided the name. Across time, Brixton became a working-class area, and was still marked by wartime bombing in 1948, when the first black faces appeared in white south London: Jamaicans from the Windrush, the very first immigrant ship from the Caribbean, who had temporary accommodation in a deep bunker in Clapham and found their way to the employment exchange in Brixton. Today, about a quarter of the local population has Caribbean or African origins, and newer arrivals from many other countries have joined them.

A bad reputation clings to Brixton. In 1981, young blacks with no good prospects in life rioted because they felt the police were discriminating against them. In 1999, a bomb planted in Electric Avenue by a neo-Nazi injured 39 people. The area still has its problems, often connected to drug dealing, but recent developments have been more encouraging. A lively cultural scene and the markets help to make Brixton an increasingly popular place.

The dreadlocks, headscarves and flowing African robes of traders and customers around Electric Avenue leave no doubt about its multicultural character. The wares include yams, plantains and manioc, dried fish from West Africa, religious items from Haiti, Chinese medicinal herbs, huge cooking pots, and bins filled with mops and brooms. Designers' shops and vintage fashion add a little hipness to the mix. In the gaudily painted market hall, salsa music booms from a Columbian butcher's stall; outside, reggae and soul send vibrations through the railway arches. In Reliance Arcade, a row of tiny hairdressers' salons, women have their hair plaited in elaborate patterns. An alternative style is close at hand: a wig shop tempts customers inside with the promise that they, too, could look like Beyoncé.

Address Electric Avenue, SW9 8JX | Transport Brixton (Northern, Victoria Line) | Opening times Daily, various times: see http://brixtonmarket.net | Tip A great variety of cheap, delicious food is on offer in the Brixton Village market hall, from Jamaican curry and Peking dumplings to sourdough pizza and gourmet burgers.

33__Fournier Street

The ghosts of Huguenots and Jewish tailors

Several rooms in the Victoria and Albert Museum are devoted to 18th-century English arts and crafts. The displays include exquisite silk fabrics, finely woven with floral patterns in delicate colours and superb Rococo embroidery. The skills to make them were brought to London by Huguenots, Protestants who were expelled from France in 1685. Many of these immigrants lived in poverty after their arrival, but hard work and talent made others wealthy. The surviving witnesses to this prosperity are solid, handsome brick houses around Fournier Street in Spitalfields. The long rows of windows in the attic storeys of such houses were installed to admit plenty of daylight for the intricate work of weaving and sewing.

After 1750, competition from Indian and French textile industries increased. Spitalfields became a poor area. The fine residences of Huguenot families were divided up into flats. In the 19th century, a new wave of immigration created a huge demand for housing: 100,000 eastern European Jews, most of them desperately poor, came to the East End, which soon became known for the quality of its Jewish tailors – and the well-lit attics were used again. When the Jewish community dispersed, immigrants from Bangladesh kept up the tradition. Shops that sold colourful saris only 15 years ago have largely given way to restaurants, but Fashion Street is home to a college of textile design, and on Sundays, young clothes designers sell their cutting-edge fashion on the Brick Lane and Spitalfields markets.

Today, the houses in Fournier Street are sought-after homes. Residents include the artists Tracy Emin and Gilbert & George. It is still worth looking out for the Huguenots' attic windows, and traces of the Jewish past remain: a closed synagogue at no. 19 Princelet Street, parallel to Fournier Street, and the lettering »S. Schwarz« on the front of no. 33.

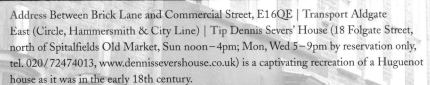

Address Between Brick Lane and Commercial Street, E1 6QE | Transport Aldgate East (Circle, Hammersmith & City Line) | Tip Dennis Severs' House (18 Folgate Street, north of Spitalfields Old Market, Sun noon–4pm; Mon, Wed 5–9pm by reservation only, tel. 020/72474013, www.dennissevershouse.co.uk) is a captivating recreation of a Huguenot house as it was in the early 18th century.

34__Freemasons' Hall

A temple of arcane mysteries

Among the patchwork of small-scale buildings in Covent Garden, a stone colossus rises abruptly above its surroundings. This is Freemasons' Hall, home of the United Grand Lodge, headquarters of British Freemasonry and a worldwide association of lodges. Although Freemasons are often regarded with suspicion as a secret society, they give a friendly welcome to all at Freemasons' Hall, displaying its opulent interior and a museum of memorabilia.

The United Grand Lodge was founded in 1717. It originally held its meetings in taverns or the halls of livery societies, until in 1776 the Freemasons built their own hall in Great Queen Street. The present building, the third, was inaugurated in 1933. Its massiveness is oppressive, both inside and outside. On the smooth stone of the façade can be seen the symbols of Freemasonry, the square and compasses. Within, dimly lit corridors painted in sombre colours lead to the museum, which expounds the history of the organisation with a display of heavy furniture, ceremonial dress and swords, glass, silver, porcelain and great numbers of medals.

Tours admit visitors to a dressing room dominated by three thrones and portraits of grand masters, who are drawn from the high aristocracy or the royal family – since 1967, a cousin of the Queen, the Duke of Kent, has held the position. The three-metre-high central throne was made in 1790 for the short, corpulent Prince Regent, who must have been a comic figure when he perched on it. A shrine to the war dead and a stained-glass memorial window representing the attainment of peace through sacrifice can be admired, before huge bronze doors open to reveal the inner sanctum: the Grand Temple with 1725 seats banked around the grand master's throne. The eye of God looks down on proceedings from a magnificent painted ceiling, and thick walls screen the ceremonies from any other eyes.

Address 60 Great Queen Street, WC2B 5AZ | **Transport** Covent Garden (Piccadilly Line) | **Opening times** Mon–Fri 10am–5pm, tours 11am, noon, 2pm, 3pm, 4pm | **Tip** A restaurant to match the Freemasons' conservative tradition is Rules (35 Maiden Lane, tel. 0207/8365314, Mon–Sat noon–11.45pm, Sun noon–10.45pm). Founded in 1798, Rules serves British food, especially game and roast beef.

35 Fulham Palace

A country seat for bishops

Does the bishop of London ever look out of his window at the densely built urban environs of his house close to St Paul's Cathedral and wish he lived in the country? Until 1975, his predecessors had a palace in peaceful green surroundings near the Thames. In the year 700, they were already lords of the manor of Fulham, which then lay a few miles west of an Anglo-Saxon settlement named Lundenwic. At some stage – the first mention dates from 1141 – the manor house in Fulham became a summer residence for the bishops, who could reach their cathedral quickly by boat. Fulham Palace was a refuge from the stench and epidemics of London, and in the 20th century it became the bishops' official residence and place of work.

The palace has had an eventful architectural history. The oldest part, the Great Hall (1495), stands in a courtyard dating from the 16th century. Two beautiful early 19th-century rooms, the library and dining room, house an exhibition about the history of the manor and the museum shop. The chapel is Victorian, with some 1950s murals and stained glass.

Ancient and rare trees beautify the park. This was originally the work of the botanist Bishop Compton (1675–1713), who collected exotic plants and was the first person in Europe to cultivate a magnolia. The gnarled holm oak, which is estimated to be 450 years old, may have been planted in the time of Bishop Grindal (1559–1570), who once presented grapes from his garden in Fulham to Queen Elizabeth. This tradition lives on in the walled garden, where the vine house has recently been restored, and a knot garden laid out in decorative shapes bounded by low box hedges in the style of Elizabethan times. On sunny days, the lawn is a popular playground and picnic spot for families. A wooden figure representing Bishop Compton looks down benignly on the fun from the »Bishop's Tree« sculpture.

Address Bishop's Avenue, Fulham, SW6 6EE | Transport Putney Bridge (District Line), then a few minutes' walk west on the bank of the Thames | Opening times Museum Mon–Thu 12.30–4.30pm, Sun noon–5pm, in winter Mon–Thu 12.30–3.30pm, Sun noon–4pm, botanical garden during daylight hours, walled garden daily 10.15am–4.15pm; for guided tours, see www.fulhampalace.org | Tip The Drawing Room Café (daily April–Oct 9.30am–5pm, Nov–March 9.30am–4pm) in the palace serves breakfast, lunch and afternoon tea in elegant rooms with comfortable armchairs or on the garden terrace.

36 The Gas Lamp in Carting Lane

Sewers and street lighting

More than 200 years after gas lighting was first introduced on London's streets, in Pall Mall in 1807, 2000 gas lamps still provide flickering illumination in areas such as Mayfair and Covent Garden. The strangest of them has burned day and night for 100 years in a ravine-like street called Carting Lane next to the Savoy Hotel. In 1894, Joseph Edmund Webb patented his »sewer gas destructor lamp«. Its purpose was to burn methane. It is sometimes said that the lamp in Carting Lane uses the vapours generated in the toilets of the luxury hotel next to it, and that the street should therefore be renamed »Farting Lane«. It is true that a sewer, to which the Savoy is connected, runs down the lane to the Embankment, but since the 1950s, the lantern has operated on normal gas.

Webb's invention was not intended to replace the gas produced from coal in a gasworks, but to have an additional safety benefit. During its operation with conventional gas, it drew explosive methane, which was a hazard to the public, out of the sewers and burned it along with the gas from the mains supply. The problem and Webb's solution were consequences of the construction of sewers in London by the engineer Joseph Bazalgette. Following the »Great Stink« in summer 1858, when the stench from the Thames made it impossible for Parliament to sit, over 400 miles of sewers were built. The system drained into the river east of London. The project included the building of the Embankment road. Two of the original pumping stations still exist: Abbey Mills to the north and Crossness to the south of the Thames, the latter a superb industrial monument with impressive cast-iron architecture. The engine there is under steam on several days a year (www.crossness.org.uk). Bazalgette's work put an end to the cholera epidemics that killed thousands of Londoners in the mid-19th century.

Address: Carting Lane (WC2R 0DW) connects the Embankment and The Strand
Transport: Embankment (Bakerloo, Circle, District, Northern Line)   On Victoria
Embankment at the end of Northumberland Avenue is a memorial to Joseph Bazalgette.

37 — The Greenwich Foot Tunnel
Under the Thames and off to Scotland

Visitors who have seen the outstanding sights in Greenwich – the National Maritime Museum, the Royal Observatory on the 0° meridian, the Queen's House and the Cutty Sark – have not exhausted all the attractions there. In a circular brick building with a glass dome close to the Cutty Sark, you can descend to a tunnel, cross under the Thames and look back over the water from Island Gardens on the north bank to the splendid architecture of Greenwich and its park.

Tunnels have been built beneath the river in many places in London. The first of them, the work of Marc Brunel and Isambard Kingdom Brunel from 1825 to 1843, connected Limehouse on the north bank with Rotherhithe on the south bank. This was also the world's first tunnel beneath a river, and more were built under the Thames in the 19th century. They served Tube trains and obviated the need for technically challenging bridges across a wide river on which tall ships sailed.

The Greenwich Foot Tunnel opened in 1902 to allow dockers to reach the warehouses and port basins on the Isle of Dogs, a peninsula on the north bank formed by a loop of the Thames. The tunnel is 15 metres below the surface and 370 metres long. It was made from cast-iron rings covered by a layer of concrete and 200,000 white tiles. Broad winding stairs lead down to it below the circular buildings at either end. Since 1904, lifts have operated. They were renewed recently, again for the benefit of those who work on the north bank – nowadays employees of financial institutions around Canary Wharf. Many go to work by bike, ignoring the instructions to dismount in the tunnel. If they don't feel like going to the office when they emerge on the north side, they can simply carry on pedalling: the tunnel is part of national cycle route no. 1, which goes all the way from the south coast at Dover to the Scottish Highlands.

Address Greenwich Foot Tunnel, SE10 9NN | Transport DLR to Island Gardens (north bank) or Cutty Sark (south bank) | Opening times 24 hours daily | Tip In The Old Brewery (café daily 10am–5pm, bar with a lovely beer garden 11am–11pm, restaurant from 6–11pm) next to the Royal Naval College, the excellent beers of the Meantime Brewing Company are on tap.

38__The Grenadier

Cosy, until the ghost appears

There are some astonishing corners of London where the feeling of being in a throbbing capital city suddenly vanishes. One such place is in Belgravia, close to the roaring traffic of Knightsbridge. Leave the imposing stone façades of Wilton Crescent for the smaller Wilton Row, then turn left – and all at once a village scene confronts you. A 300-year-old pub beneath trees is painted in patriotic red, white and blue. The inn sign depicts a soldier in a bearskin cap, and a bright red sentry box stands to the left of the steps that lead up to the front door.

The Grenadier Guards, founded in 1656 as a bodyguard for King Charles II, were stationed in a barracks on this site until 1818. In that year, the officers' mess was converted into a pub, and little has changed since. The bar in the wood-panelled room at the front has its original pewter top. In the Wellington Room behind, hearty pub meals are served. Photos, prints and newspaper cuttings on the walls celebrate military tradition and the pub itself: Grenadier Guards pose for a snapshot in front of Buckingham Palace, and an old print shows a Waterloo Dinner, the annual celebration of Napoleon's defeat that was given by the Duke of Wellington for his comrades nearby in his London residence.

It is likely that the Duke himself drank here with his officers. Their carousals were not always marked by good behaviour. During one drinking bout, a subaltern is said to have been caught cheating at cards. His comrades beat him so savagely that he died on the cobblestones in front of the pub. More details are not known, but the incident is thought to have happened in September. In this month an icy chill is reported to haunt the building. Footsteps and groans can be heard, and a mysterious figure moves silently through the rooms. The banknotes that guests have signed and pinned to the ceiling of the front bar are meant to propitiate the ghost.

Address 18 Wilton Row, SW1X 7NR | **Transport** Hyde Park Corner (Piccadilly Line) | **Opening times** Mon–Sun noon–11pm | **Tip** Apsley House (Hyde Park Corner, April–Oct Wed–Sun 11am–5pm, Nov–March Sat–Sun 10am–4pm) has a fine interior, an exquisite art collection and memorabilia from the first Duke of Wellington's military career.

39__Hawksmoor's Pyramid
An enigma in the churchyard

St Anne's Church in Limehouse is one of 50 that were to be constructed for the growing population of London according to an act of Parliament in 1711. Only twelve were built, six of them by Nicholas Hawksmoor (1661–1736), who had worked under the aegis of Sir Christopher Wren on St Paul's Cathedral, Chelsea Hospital and Hampton Court Palace.

Hawksmoor evolved his own idiosyncratic interpretation of the Baroque style, revealing his interest in Gothic and classical architecture and his liking for dramatic effects of light and dark, mass and space. The striking tower of St Anne's Church has outsized corner buttresses and a top storey turned by 45 degrees. The clock, the highest on a London church, used to chime the quarter hours for ships in the surrounding docks, as the tower was within sight of the official time signal in Greenwich. Small pyramids surmount the east end of St Anne's.

In the large churchyard stand tall plane trees, benches, scattered gravestones and a three-metre-high stone pyramid, partly covered in moss and lichen. The south side bears the inscription »The Wisdom of Solomon« and a weathered coat of arms on which it is just possible to make out a unicorn. In the absence of hard evidence on the origin of the pyramid, speculation has run riot. Its dimensions do not fit the most popular theory, that it was destined for the church tower. Two prominent contemporary authors associated with London, Peter Ackroyd and Ian Sinclair, have woven stories around a possible connection to the occult. Are Hawksmoor's six churches located in the form of a pentagram? Is there a mystic background to the architect's known fascination with geometry? Does the pyramid in some way express the beliefs of Freemasons? Or is it simply a leftover architectural component that fitted nowhere and has remained to adorn and add atmosphere to the churchyard? Nobody knows.

Address Newell Street, E14 7HP | Transport Limehouse (DLR) | Opening times
Churchyard open in daylight hours | Tip The actor Sir Ian McKellen owns a historic
pub that serves food on the banks of the Thames in Limehouse: The Grapes (76 Narrow
Street, tel. 020/79874396).

40 Holland Park

More than a Dutch garden

In the north-west of Holland Park, two huge bronze tortoises crawl beneath the style of a sundial. The work of the sculptor Wendy Taylor, they could be a metaphor for the way that changes sometimes happen very slowly.

Until 1952, this 23-hectare park in the middle of the city was the private property of an aristocratic family. 400 years ago, Sir Walter Cope, chancellor of the exchequer under King James I, built himself a mansion here in wooded grounds more than two miles west of the City of London. The house later passed into the possession of the earls of Holland and was named Holland House. The estate included pasture land as well as the woods and gardens around the mansion. For 100 years from the mid-18th century, Holland House was a meeting place for high society and politicians, where the great parliamentarian Charles James Fox spent much of his childhood. The illustrious visitors included Sir Walter Scott, Lord Byron and Charles Dickens. Then the building fell into disrepair, suffered severe bomb damage in the Second World War, and was sold by the owners to the Royal Borough of Kensington and Chelsea.

Over decades, the ruins of Holland House and its grounds became one of London's finest parks. The east wing of the house was saved and made into a youth hostel. The Dutch Garden that survived from the days of glamour was restored, and now presents a blaze of colour in summer. The Japanese-style Kyoto Garden with its flowering cherry trees, magnolias and cedars was added. In the wooded northern section of the park, daffodils and rhododendrons flower in spring. There is a café and covered arcades for rainy days. Tennis courts, children's playgrounds, open-air chess and opera performances beneath a canopy provide entertainment. Thus an aristocratic estate became a place of recreation for one and all, and backpackers sleep in the remains of the mansion.

Address Abbotsbury Road, W8 6LU | Transport Holland Park (Central Line) | Opening times Mon–Sun 7.30am until 30 minutes before dusk | Tip In 1866, the artist Lord Leighton built himself a fine dwelling and studio with an opulent Moorish-style interior (Leighton House, 12 Holland Park Road, daily except Tue 10am–5.30pm). The gardens and houses of an artists' colony in the neighbouring streets are also a fine sight.

41__Horse at Water

A restful sight at Marble Arch

The north-east corner of Hyde Park is a spot that has seen its share of uproar. On Sundays, any eccentric or hothead with firm opinions and a loud voice can harangue the public at Speaker's Corner. Countless criminals were hanged on Tyburn gallows. Now the name of the place derives from a triumphal arch of Carrara marble. It was designed by John Nash as an entrance to Buckingham Palace, but had to be moved when the palace was extended in 1851 – the famous balcony for royal waving marks the approximate site. In contrast to public executions and the Sunday shouting, a bronze sculpture of a horse's head now imparts a soothing mood to Marble Arch.

The sculptor Nic Fiddian-Green has loved the form of a horse's head since he was young. His first inspiration was a work in the British Museum, the horse of the moon goddess Selene from the sculptures on the pediment of the Parthenon. Today Fiddian-Green's outsized horses' heads have been installed in many different countries. »Horse at Water«, placed between a 1960s fountain and Nash's arch in 2010, is ten metres high and weighs 17 tons. In what appears to be a miraculous balancing act, it rises above a flat metal base that represents the surface of the water from which the horse is drinking.

Traffic thunders all around, as Marble Arch is one big roundabout for buses, but the horse's head is a perfect motif to make a transition from the surrounding bustle to Hyde Park. Horses have a close historic connection with the park: Hyde Park Barracks is the base of the Household Cavalry regiment, which rides daily to the changing of the guard on Horse Guards' Parade and has ceremonial functions at royal occasions. The park was once the place for fine ladies to show themselves in their carriages, and the broad track called Rotten Row that forms the southern boundary of the park is still used by riders.

Address North-east corner of Hyde Park, W1H 7AL | Transport Marble Arch (Central Line) | Tip The Serpentine Gallery and Serpentine Sackler Gallery in Kensington Gardens (Tue – Sun 10am – 6pm) put on changing exhibitions of contemporary art. Each year a renowned architect is invited to design a temporary Serpentine Pavilion.

42___James Smith & Sons
Where a gentleman buys his umbrella

Is there a lovelier shop front anywhere in London? Above windows framed in dark wood, the name »James Smith & Sons – Established 1830« is announced with a flourish. The initials are radiant in red and gold, and the strip of brass beneath with beaten lettering still has a shine. The signage advertises products that sound like props from a Victorian murder mystery: »life preservers, dagger canes, sword-sticks« above one window, »riding crops, whips, Irish blackthorns« next to it. Sticks are still sold here, but umbrellas are the mainstay of the business.

James Smith founded his shop in Foubert Place, Soho, and manu-factured umbrellas in a workshop at the back. In 1857, he moved to the present address in New Oxford Street, where there is still a re-pair shop in the cellar. In those days, every gentleman carried a stick, whether a white cane or something more rustic for days in the coun-try. Umbrellas became increasingly common in Europe from the 17th century, but the first man to carry one in England regularly did so surprisingly late, from about 1750. He was regularly pelted with mud by coachmen and sedan-chair bearers, who thought the invention a threat to their business.

At James Smith, still a family-run company, the interior lives up to the façade. Above the counter, a gallery with a glass balustrade serves as the accounts department. The wooden shop fittings of drawers and cupboards are 150 years old. They display a fine prod-uct range: umbrellas with the head of Sherlock Holmes or a duck on the handle, conservative models all in black, floral patterns and lace for ladies, folding umbrellas in gaudy colours. The sticks come with a huge variety of knobs, and even integrated corkscrews or whisky flasks. Every wish can be fulfilled, but the management does issue one warning: »It is inadvisable to lend your James Smith umbrella to even your closest friend.«

43___Jamme Masjid Mosque
A house of three religions

The building at the north-west corner of Brick Lane and Fournier Street has a remarkable history. Today it stands in »Banglatown« – the marketing name for the rows of curry houses at the southern end of Brick Lane. This district, Spitalfields, belongs to Tower Hamlets borough, where almost 40 per cent of the population are of Bangladeshi origin. During the 1970s, as their numbers increased in the East End, they founded several mosques, one of them in an existing place of worship.

Spitalfields was an immigrant quarter 300 years ago. Huguenots, that is Protestants who had been expelled from France, settled here and built a church on Brick Lane in 1743. In time the Huguenot community was assimilated and lost its distinct identity. In 1809 the church was made over to a society for converting Jews to Christianity. This mission was unsuccessful, and after only ten years the building became a Methodist chapel. In the late 19th century, tens of thousands of Jews from eastern Europe moved into the area and converted the old church into the Machzeike Hadass Synagogue in 1898. In the following decades Spitalfields was a poor but lively Jewish quarter. After the Second World War the Jewish community gradually moved away, and the synagogue building was shut up. It reopened in 1976 as the Jamme Masjid Mosque.

A tall, shining cylinder of steel that glows in changing colours at night, a substitute for a minaret, is the outward sign that a third religion has now taken possession. Inside the building, the old church pews were removed, the upper galleries in the prayer hall enlarged, and basins for ritual ablutions installed. A survival from the first church is a sundial on the Fournier Street side, inscribed »umbra summus«: »we are shadows«. This reference to the insubstantiality of human life raises the question: is the mosque the final chapter in this story?

Address Brick Lane, E1 6QL | Transport Aldgate East (Circle, Hammersmith & City Line) | Tip The few traces of Jewish culture in this area include a 24-hour bagel shop (Beigel Bake, 159 Brick Lane) and a synagogue in Sandy's Row, an alley south of Spitalfields Market.

44 Jean Cocteau's Murals in Notre Dame

The sixth-largest French city is Londres

France and England are bound together by centuries of friendship and hostility, mutual admiration and distrust. The English cross the Channel in search of French joie de vivre and cuisine. French people have taken refuge in England and founded their own institutions there – for example the church of Notre Dame de la France in a shabby alley behind Leicester Square. It was built in 1865 for the numerous poor French residents of Soho, destroyed in the Second World War, and reconstructed in 1955. A shallow dome admits light to the circular interior, where monastic singing from concealed speakers cannot quite drown out the snoring of the homeless who come here to sleep on the benches. One feature of the church that makes a visit worthwhile are the murals painted by the film director and artist Jean Cocteau, now behind glass in a chapel. With vigorous lines and subdued colours, he painted a Crucifixion on which only Christ's legs can be seen.

French influence in Soho has deep roots, including influxes of refugees during the revolution of 1789. In the war, the French House pub (49 Dean Street) was a rendezvous for supporters of Charles de Gaulle. Today the French quartier is South Kensington, where a lycée, the Institut français, a librairie française and French cafés lie close to the Tube station. Gallic presence is noticeable all over London, however, as the French population of the city is estimated at 400,000. Many of the younger ones work in hotels and restaurants as a way to learn English. Others earn high salaries in the City, or are attracted by London's creative scene for design and new media. This means that Londres now has more French residents than Bordeaux, and vote-catching politicians come over from Paris during election campaigns.

Address Leicester Place, WC2H 7RN | **Transport** Leicester Square (Northern, Piccadilly Line) | **Opening times** Mon–Sun 9.30am–9pm | **Tip** Maison Bertaux (28 Greek Street), founded in 1871, is London's oldest French patisserie in London.

45 __ The Jewel Tower
Democracy, weights and measures

The official name for the buildings of Parliament is the »Palace of Westminster« because a royal palace once stood there. It was built in the mid-11th century for King Edward the Confessor and remained a royal residence until 1529. The most impressive survivor of the medieval palace, Westminster Hall, dates from 1099 and was given its magnificent hammer-beam roof 300 years later. There is also a smaller, less well-known relic of the old Westminster Palace: the Jewel Tower.

This stone tower was constructed in about 1365 as a safe place to keep the precious robes, jewels, gold and silver of the royal treasury. Later it was the home of the parliamentary archive, and from the 1860s until 1938, it housed the Standards Department, the government body responsible for weights and measures, as its thick walls and the constant temperature inside were ideal for making exact measurements and keeping the standard weights.

Today, the Jewel Tower is separated from the rest of the parliament by a busy road. It stands among lawns and the remains of a moat. The three-storey tower is well worth visiting for the exhibition Parliament Past and Present. The displays show the appearance of the old Palace of Westminster and St Stephen's Chapel, where the House of Commons met, and tell of the construction of the present Houses of Parliament in the 19th century after a devastating fire in 1834. In times when it is easy to be cynical about politics, the part of the exhibition that outlines the long road to democracy is uplifting and encouraging. It is a sober and well-presented account of the first councils of nobles and the emergence of the House of Commons in the Middle Ages, the defeat of attempts to establish an absolute monarchy, the struggles for freedom of the press and votes for women – a history to be proud of, whatever the latest headlines from Westminster happen to be.

Address Abingdon Street, SW1P 3JX | Transport Westminster (Circle, District, Jubilee Line) | Opening times April–Oct Mon–Sun 10am–5pm; Nov–March Sat, Sun 10am–4pm | Tip Parliament, including the magnificent House of Lords and Westminster Hall, is open for guided tours on Saturdays and Mon–Fri when Parliament is not sitting. See www.parliament.uk/visiting or tel. 020 7219 4114

46__The K2 Telephone Kiosk

The prototype of a famous design

Behind the wrought-iron gates of the Royal Academy of Arts stands the very first example of the red telephone box called K2. This one-off item was made of wood for a competition in 1924, as the earlier model, K1, had been rejected.

The designer of K2 was Giles Gilbert Scott (1880–1960), a scion of a well-known dynasty of architects. At the age of 22, he was awarded the commission to build the Anglican Cathedral in Liverpool, and has a strong presence on the Thames with his two unmistakable power stations at Bankside (now the Tate Modern) and Battersea. For the miniature architecture of the phone box, Scott turned to the formal repertoire of classical building. His careful design gave it a shallow dome and fluted window frames. For the colour, he proposed silver, but the General Post Office opted for red and installed 1700 steel-built K2 phone kiosks, one of which stands opposite the prototype. The 200 surviving K2s are all protected monuments.

With its height of 2.74 metres and a weight of 1250 kilos, K2 was too expensive, but alternatives made of concrete (K3) with a built-in stamp vending machine (K4), and of plywood (K5) failed to catch on. In 1935, Scott produced a simplified version: K6, 30 centimetres shorter and 500 kilos lighter than K2, with a teak door. 60,000 of them were manufactured. K6 is plainer and has eight rows of windows on each side, with the middle window in each row wider (K2 has six rows of three windows, all the same size). K6 became a design classic, so popular that its successor, K8, did not appear until 1968. 11,000 K6 boxes still stand in Britain, and a considerable number can be seen abroad. 2260 of them are listed heritage structures. They are not all identical. Look out for the crown in the pediment: since 1953, it has been a depiction of St Edward's Crown, the one used for coronations, rather than a stylised »Tudor« crown.

Address Burlington House, Piccadilly, W1J 0BD | **Transport** Piccadilly Circus (Bakerloo, Piccadilly Line) | **Tip** The Royal Academy of Arts founded in 1768 has its own art collection and puts on outstanding changing exhibitions. Its cafés are good places to take a break.

47 The Kindertransport Monument

The place where 10,000 Jewish children arrived

The group of bronze figures in front of the south entrance to Liverpool Street Station depicts five children of various ages. The youngest, a girl, sits on a suitcase with a teddy bear in her hand. The boy to her right holds a satchel and a violin case. The older girl behind him is not keeping an eye on the smaller ones at this moment, as they are all looking in different directions. They are waiting to be collected, and the group is about to split up. The names of cities on a length of railway track behind them show the children's places of origins: on one side »Cologne – Hanover – Nuremberg – Stuttgart – Düsseldorf – Frankfurt – Bremen – Munich«, on the other »Danzig – Breslau – Prague – Hamburg – Mannheim – Leipzig – Berlin – Vienna«.

Between December 1938 and September 1939, almost 10,000 Jewish children arrived at Liverpool Street via the Netherlands and the port of Harwich. Following the attacks on synagogues and German Jews instigated by the Nazi government on the »Kristallnacht« (»night of broken glass«), 9 to 10 November 1938, the British government allowed Jewish children up to the age of 17 to immigrate, provided that a foster family and a benefactor willing to give a bond of 50 pounds were found. The first to come were 196 children from an orphanage that had been burned down in Berlin. The German authorities allowed the children to take one suitcase and one bag, containing no valuables and only one photo. No adult escort and no farewells at the railway station were permitted. The 10,000 children were dispersed around Britain, and few ever saw their parents again.

Frank Weisler, who was born in Danzig (now Gdansk) in 1929 and came to his grandmother in London with a Kindertransport, later studied architecture in Manchester and became a sculptor in Israel. He made the monument in London and similar works in Hoek van Holland, Gdansk and Berlin.

Address Hope Square, EC2M 7QN, in front of Liverpool Street Station | Transport Liverpool Street (Central, Circle, District, Hammersmith & City, Metropolitan Line) | Tip More information can be found on the website www.kindertransport.org. W. G. Sebald, a German writer who spent most of his life in England, made it the subject of his strange and brilliant novel »Austerlitz«.

48_Leadenhall Market

Romans, cheesemongers, bankers

700 years after the first mention of a market on this spot, Leadenhall Market seems out of place among the bank towers and right next to the high-tech Lloyds Building. It is a magnificent piece of 19th-century ostentation by Sir Horace Jones, architect and surveyor to the City of London, who designed Smithfield meat market, Billingsgate fish market and Tower Bridge.

The architecture of Leadenhall Market is full of sumptuous detail. At its main entrance is a stone pediment with urns and scrolls, dragons flanking a fine clock, and the motto of the City of London: »Domine dirige nos«, »Guide us, Lord«. Inside, a high roof of cast iron and glass covers two main arcades and passages leading from them where market stalls are still set up on weekdays. The walls of the permanent shops are painted in Burgundy red and cream, while the plasterwork between the windows depicts orange trees growing in pots. The iron construction with its fluted columns, garlands in Ionic capitals and silver dragons breathing fire from every corner, is an exuberant demonstration of Victorian abhorrence of the purely functional.

The market had more modest origins, of course. By the year 1321, poultry traders were meeting around a dwelling called Leadenhall – the name probably indicates that this building had an expensive roof. They were soon joined by cheesemongers, and Leadenhall evolved into a place where wool, leather goods, cutlery, meat and vegetables were sold. Following the Great Fire of 1666, the market was given a roof for the first time, and in 1881 the present market replaced the old structures. Commercial activity has been going on here for even longer than the recorded history of the market: in Roman times, this was the site of the forum and the basilica, a large hall used for courts of law, assemblies and trading. Today, the shoppers here are mainly employed in the finance business.

Address Gracechurch Street, EC3V 1LR | Transport Monument (Circle, District Line) |
Opening times Mon–Fri 10am–6pm; the hours of individual shops and restaurants in the
market vary | Tip To shop and eat more cheaply than in the finance district, head east for
ten minutes along Leadenhall Street and Aldgate to Whitechapel High Street.

49__Liberty

Heart of oak are our shops

… well, actually »our ships« is the correct version of the song, but perhaps the Royal Navy will forgive this paraphrase of its official march, as Liberty is almost literally a flagship store. In the 1920s, when the shop had outgrown its premises on Regent Street, an extension was built around the corner in Great Marlborough Street using the wood from its two last wooden warships, HMS Impregnable and HMS Hindustan.

By this time, the department store founded by Arthur Lasenby Liberty in 1875 had long been an institution in London, and had even made its mark on the international art scene: »Stile Liberty«, the Italian expression for Art Nouveau, is derived from the style that the store championed. Liberty worked with leading designers of the Arts & Crafts and Art Nouveau movements to create furniture, lamps, carpets and clothes that expressed modern lifestyle in the late 19th century. The company's proprietary textile patterns from that period are still popular on cushions, curtains, bags, men's ties, and a host of other items.

The 1920s façade, the length of HMS Hindustan, is a charming piece of architectural nostalgia in half-timbered, black-and-white Tudor Revival style. Naval timbers were also recycled inside the shop as wooden panelling. Three roofed courtyards with galleries on four storeys around a light well recreate the atmosphere of a historic inn or a comfortable country house. There are leaded windows and stone fireplaces, woodcarvings on the door frames and balustrades, a hammer-beam roof and even linen-fold panelling in the lifts. The fabrics department is legendary, the carpet department an Aladdin's cave. However, Liberty is not a museum, but remains an innovative company that collaborates with 21st-century designers such as the cross-dressing ceramic artist Grayson Perry and exploits its unsinkable brand name to the full.

Address 210–220 Regent Street, W1B 5AH | Transport Oxford Circus (Bakerloo, Central, Victoria Line) | Opening times Mon–Sat 10am–8pm, Sun noon–6pm | Tip A walk along crowded Oxford Street and Regent Street is hard work, but from the top deck of a bus you can either look down on the retail scrum or up at opulent shop fronts that were built to impress with mosaics, carved stone and metalwork.

50 _ Lincoln's Inn
A tranquil refuge for lawyers

To pass through the gateway on Chancery Lane is to leave the noise of London behind and to step into an older, quieter world. Mature plane trees spread their boughs over beautifully kept lawns. A varied ensemble of historic buildings borders courtyards where the atmosphere is reminiscent of an ancient university – and indeed Lincoln's Inn, one of four institutions of the legal profession that possess their own enclave in central London, was once a place where law students lived. Those who wish to qualify as a barrister must be members of these »inns of court«, which are a kind of professional association whose responsibilities include training young lawyers. Like the nearby Gray's Inn, Inner Temple and Middle Temple, Lincoln's Inn is home to barristers' chambers and collegiate institutions such as a chapel, hall and library.

Lincoln's Inn is first mentioned in documents in 1422, but probably existed decades earlier. The gatehouse dates from 1520, the Old Hall, which is used for meals, debates and festivities, from the year 1490. The scholar and Lord Chancellor of England Thomas More, who enrolled in 1496, is one of many eminent persons who dined in this hall. Five prime ministers – Pitt the Younger, Gladstone, Asquith, Thatcher and Blair – were members of Lincoln's Inn. Visitors can walk in the courtyards but not enter the buildings with the exception of the Gothic chapel, completed in 1623 and restored 60 years later by Wren, also a member of the Inn. It became an early casualty of air warfare in 1915, when bombs dropped from a zeppelin destroyed two stained-glass windows. The Stone Buildings in classical style running north along Chancery Lane date mainly from the 18th century, the red-brick segment of the library and Great Hall from the 19th century. These parts combine to form a harmonious ensemble, and a refreshing contrast to the neighbouring streets.

Address Chancery Lane, WC2A 3TL | Transport Chancery Lane (Central Line) | Opening times Courtyards Mon–Fri 7am–7pm, chapel Mon–Fri 9am–5pm | Tip Dealers in the bazaar-like subterranean Silver Vaults sell an extraordinary range of silver products, some of them extremely precious (53–64 Chancery Lane, Mon–Fri 9am–5.30pm, Sat 9am–1pm).

51 The Lloyd's Building
Futuristic, yet a monument

It is rare for a building less than 30 years old to be listed by English Heritage as one of half a million protected monuments. And for a work by a living architect to be included among the 10,000 structures that are officially designated as grade one, i.e. »of exceptional interest«, is not merely unusual, but unique. Richard Rogers achieved this distinction with his Lloyd's Building of 1986, which gained grade-one listing in 2011.

Seen from Leadenhall Street, the Lloyd's Building towers above its neighbours and rebukes their conservative, early 20th-century stone façades with expanses of grey metal. External glass lifts, water pipes and ventilation ducts rise up the shiny surface, and conspicuous blue cranes for the window cleaners perch on the roof. The design principle is that of the Centre Pompidou in Paris, which made Rogers and his former partner Renzo Piano famous: everything that is hidden in conventional architecture – lifts, staircases, the building services – is boldly displayed on the outside, in order to create an uncluttered, adaptable interior space.

When it was inaugurated, the 88-metre-high building (95 metres with the cranes) was all the more provocative for being the new home of a revered 300-year-old institution. Lloyd's of London evolved from Lloyd's Coffee House, which by 1688 had become a place for merchants and sea captains to exchange news and, increasingly, to conclude insurance agreements. Lloyd's is not a company but an association of independent insurers. Trading is done on the ground floor of a 60-metre-high atrium, around which three office towers and three towers for building utilities are grouped. The interior is by no means entirely high-tech in appearance: the Committee Room on the 11th floor, originally a dining room designed by the great 18th-century architect Robert Adam, was transferred here from the old Lloyd's Building.

Address 1 Lime Street, EC3M 7HA | Transport Monument (Circle, District Line) | Opening times Open only during the Open House Weekend in September; for a virtual tour, see www.lloyds.com | Tip Opposite the Lloyd's Building stands a new high-profile work by Rogers, the 224-metre Leadenhall Building (2014), known as the »Cheesegrater« thanks to its sloping façades.

52 London Stone

A mythical stone in shabby surroundings

Neglected and disregarded, the supposed foundation stone of a great metropolis lies behind bars and dirty glass in the façade of a down-at-heel 1960s office block. By crouching and peering through, it is possible to see a fragment of limestone measuring about 50 by 40 by 30 centimetres – all that remains of London Stone, which was once larger and is associated in legend with the beginnings of the city.

According to one story, it is a relic of the stone circle built by the giants Gog and Magog on the site now occupied by St Paul's Cathedral. A 12th-century chronicle tells that Brutus came to London from the ruins of Troy and was instructed by the goddess Diana to build a temple, of which London Stone was the altar. The mystic poet William Blake believed that druids performed human sacrifices on the stone. Others claimed that King Arthur drew the sword Excalibur from it, while New Agers of modern times take it to be the mid-point of a ley line connecting St Paul's with the Tower of London. A more sober interpretation sees the block as the central Roman milestone from which distances were measured.

The facts are scanty. The first written reference dates from the 11th century. In the Middle Ages great significance was ascribed to the stone: debts were paid and oaths taken there. It was the landmark at which the rebel Jack Cade claimed to be ruler of London in 1450. Until the road was widened in 1742, London Stone stood on the south side of the street, was then placed in the wall of St Swithin's Church and survived the destruction of the church in 1941.

The site of St Swithin's is now 111 Cannon Street. In the sports shop which occupied the ground floor until recently, the stone was visible behind glass. Now a newsagent conceals it behind a display of magazines. As part of plans to develop the site, proposals have been made to move the stone. In a city that is proud of its traditions, this strange item deserves a more worthy setting.

Address 111 Cannon Street, EC4N 5BP | Transport Cannon Street (Circle, District Line) | Tip Sir Christopher Wren was the architect of St Stephen Walbrook (39 Walbrook, Mon–Fri 10am–4pm), a church with a dome that that may have served as a trial run for St Paul's Cathedral. The lovely interior is noteworthy for a controversial altar sculpted by Henry Moore.

53_Lord's Cricket Ground

A sacred site for fans of the summer sport

Wembley for football, Wimbledon for tennis, Lord's for cricket. Lord's is older than the other two, as the first recorded match here took place on 22 June 1814. 200 years ago, aristocrats liked to play cricket and wagered enormous sums of money on the outcome. From 1787, the businessman Thomas Lord made ground available for this purpose on the site that is now Dorset Square. Later he moved to a place south-east of the present stadium, but had to make way for the new Regent's Canal. The third Lord's, »the home of cricket«, is for the most part a nondescript modern structure – with two notable exceptions. The Media Centre, a great viewing pod that was built in boatyards using marine technology, won the Stirling Prize for Architecture in 1999. The splendid Pavilion at the opposite end dates from 1890. Here, club members watch matches from the tiered balconies, or through the windows of the venerable Long Room beneath portraits of great cricketers of the past. Many members proudly wear the red-and-yellow (»bacon and egg«) striped blazer of the ground's owner, the Marylebone Cricket Club. When rain stops play, they can see the treasures in the world's oldest sports museum, including a stuffed sparrow that was hit by a ball in 1936, and the small urn containing the »ashes of English cricket«, a trophy made in 1882 following a catastrophic defeat at the hands of the Australian team.

Although the number 111 has a special aura – Tolkien's »Lord of the Rings« opens with Bilbo Baggins' eleventy-first birthday party, for example – in cricket it is unlucky, and is called a »Nelson« because Admiral Nelson is said to have had one arm, one eye and one leg (in fact he had two legs). When the score of a team or batsman is 111, or 222 or 333, the superstitious expect disaster. To avert misfortune, the umpire David Shepherd used to stand on one leg if this score was reached.

Address St John's Wood Road, NW8 8QN | **Transport** St John's Wood (Jubilee Line) | **Tip** A pleasant stroll along the Regent's Canal, which can be reached 400 metres south or east of Lord's, leads west to the canal basin at Little Venice or east to Regent's Park.

54 MI6 Headquarters
James Bond's office

Bond is no pen-pusher, but sometimes he has to go to the office. In a fortress-like building on the banks of the Thames next to Vauxhall Bridge, he is briefed by M, the head of the Secret Intelligence Service (often still given its old name: MI6). Although the secret service has been carrying out operations abroad since 1909, the government did not officially admit its existence until 1994. Only one year later the organisation, or at least its architectural façade, was on public view thanks to a new headquarters designed by Terry Farrell which is known internationally through its appearances in the Bond films such as »The World is Not Enough«.

Solid fences and a host of cameras protect the building. Green-tinted windows – 27 different kinds of protective glass are said to have been used – give nothing away to prying eyes. A stacked-up design with projections and terraces mitigates the structure's bulk and has drawn comparisons with a ziggurat or an Aztec temple. Nevertheless, the building has a massive, hostile, closed-off presence. Of course it is well protected against bugging and other dangers. In 2000, a hit by an anti-tank missile, probably fired by the »Real IRA«, failed to cause much damage. There are rumours of a tunnel beneath the Thames to government departments in Westminster.

The riverbank location is a surprising and likeable touch. The long-distance Thames Path passes directly in front, allowing walkers to wave at the cameras. The perfect contrast to the smooth beige surfaces above are the rough stones of the quayside, covered in green water weed and adorned by lions' heads with heavy iron rings in their jaws. At low tide you can walk across a gravel beach and see, directly beneath the MI6 building, a dark gate with hanging chains in the embankment wall. This is the outlet for storm flooding of an underground watercourse, the River Effra. The weak point that Bond's enemies are seeking?

Address 85 Vauxhall Cross, Albert Embankment, SE1 7TP | Transport Vauxhall (Victoria Line) | Opening times None, it goes without saying | Tip As British as Bond: the Tate Britain at the other end of Vauxhall Bridge is the repository of the national collection of British painting (daily 10am–6pm).

55__The Monument

When 13,000 houses burned down

The legacy of London's worst disaster is a memorial whose uniqueness at the time of completion in 1677 is demonstrated by its simple name: The Monument. It is 202 feet (61 metres) high and stands exactly 202 feet from the spot in Pudding Lane where a blaze broke out in a bakery on 2 September 1666. When the »Great Fire« finally burned out after five days, half of the city was a field of smouldering ruins. 13,000 houses, 89 churches and St Paul's Cathedral were destroyed. 100,000 citizens lost their homes.

Sir Christopher Wren, the architect of 50 churches and the new St Paul's after the fire, also received the commission for The Monument. He designed a limestone column five metres in diameter capped by a flaming urn of gilded copper. Within the column, 311 steps wind up to the viewing platform. The base bears Latin inscriptions and relief carvings: on the east side they record details of The Monument itself, the south face is a verbose glorification of King Charles II, and the west side is devoted to an allegorical depiction of the ruined and the restored City of London, showing the king as a victorious Roman. A close look at the north side reveals that the bottom line of an inscription has been deleted. The Monument was built at a time of anti-Catholic hysteria following false accusations of a conspiracy to assassinate the king. According to the inscription, which was removed in 1830, the Great Fire had been put out, »but Popish frenzy, which wrought such horrors, is not yet quenched«.

The Monument is hemmed in all around by office blocks, but the effort of climbing to the top is worthwhile, as its immediate neighbours are lower, and a gap has been left towards the river. To the east, you get a view of the Tower of London and Tower Bridge, to the south the glass spike of The Shard, to the north the bank towers, and to the west St Paul's Cathedral and Westminster.

Address Monument Street, EC3R 6DB | **Transport** Monument (Circle, District Line) | **Opening times** Mon–Sun 9.30am–5.30pm | **Tip** The Great Fire started in Pudding Lane and stopped at Pie Corner, the junction of Cock Lane and Giltspur Street, which is marked by a gilded cherub. The walk there from The Monument via King William Street, Poultry, Cheapside and Newgate Street shows the extent of the devastation.

56_Mudchute City Farm

Animals for urban children

When children from the East End were evacuated to the country during the Second World War, shocking ignorance came to light. Some of them were amazed at the size of cows, which they had imagined to be no bigger than dogs. Today they are better informed, as London is blessed with a number of educational farmyards, of which Mudchute City Farm on the Isle of Dogs is the largest at 13 hectares.

The curious name »Mudchute« goes back to the 19th century, when docks were built in the north of the Isle of Dogs. The soil and Thames mud excavated during this work were deposited on the southern part of the peninsula, creating an unplanned but extremely fertile biotope. The port area has now become part of the shiny new Docklands with its towers for financial institutions and expensive apartments at Canary Wharf and Canada Water. The district to the south of it, formerly housing for dockers and their families, was redeveloped, and the mud heaps were converted to a park and farmyard in the 1970s.

As you walk southwards from the Crossharbour stop on the Docklands Light Railway, the scene changes completely within a few minutes. The postmodern high-rise architecture recedes into the background, meadows appear, hedgerows line the path, and you have soon reached Mudchute City Farm, where admission is free. It has pens for donkeys, sheep and llamas and a pond for geese and ducks. Turkeys wander about with impressive dangling wattles, golden pheasants strut in their cages, and horses graze in a paddock. For smaller children, there are rabbits, guinea pigs and a playground, for the older ones a riding school, and a café caters to the parents. Greedy goats are hand-fed on carrots, and various events familiarise the young generation with life on a farm – valuable entertainment and education, as the Isle of Dogs is a district where poor families live.

Address Pier Street, E143HP | Transport Crossharbour (DLR); from the station walk across the supermarket car park | Opening times Park always open, farm Mon–Sun 9am–5pm | Tip From the next DLR station, Island Gardens, it is a short walk to the river bank for a fantastic view of historic Greenwich.

57___Neal's Yard
Alternative lifestyle and Monty Python

Between 1974, when the fruit, vegetable and flower markets moved out, and the 1980s, when Covent Garden began to attract fashionable shops and crowds of tourists - at a time, that is, when the area was still pleasantly shabby and rents were low, unconventional people breathed new life into a triangular back yard. The warehouses in Neal's Yard had served the flower market and were still home to a company that made theatrical weapons and armour.

In 1978, an organic bakery with a café opened in Neal's Yard. It was joined by a cheese shop and Neal's Yard Remedies, which sold natural cosmetics and health products. Soon the courtyard had become the little island of alternative lifestyle that it still is today. The brick warehouse walls have been painted in gaudy colours – purple, orange, bright yellow – and are adorned with African masks. Tables at which diners wait for their rice-flour pizza to be served have been placed around old metal barrels planted with bamboo and shrubs. Health and beauty treatments with a mystic touch are available in the Holistic Room, the hairdresser specialises in dreadlocks, and courses about how to gather wild food in woodlands and pastures can be booked.

Neal's Yard Remedies, now a retail chain, is still present, and the Neal's Yard Dairy, sourcing artisan cheesemakers, has moved around the corner into Short's Gardens. In its early days, the shop struggled to gain a good reputation. John Cleese came in one day to find empty shelves. Production problems meant that yoghurt was on sale, but no cheese at all. The creative result of this mishap was Monty Python's celebrated cheese-shop sketch. A plaque in the yard records that »Monty Python lived here«. The recent opening of a chic wine bar in Neal's Yard, however, suggests that the spreading commercialisation of Covent Garden may soon overpower the green, alternative ethos of this enclave.

Address Between Short's Gardens and Monmouth Street, WC2H 9AT | Transport Covent Garden (Piccadilly Line) | Tip Those who prefer traditional British fare to vegetarian whole-food will find excellent fish & chips at the Rock and Sole Plaice (47 Endell Street, Mon–Sat 11.30am–11.30pm, Sun noon–10pm). The Monty Python sketch is on YouTube.

58___The Niche from Old London Bridge

Stones that were admitted to hospital

One of the few remaining fragments of London Bridge is a semi-circular covered niche with a bench. It stands in the courtyard of Guy's Hospital and has a permanent occupant – the poet John Keats, who studied medicine here and, cast in bronze, now pores over his books between the flower beds.

This weather-beaten little structure is not part of the medieval fabric of the bridge, but dates from restoration work in 1760. Until that date, shops and houses crowded the length of the bridge and limited the width of the road. These additions were then removed, and 14 niches were added to provide shelter for pedestrians. When Old London Bridge was finally demolished in 1831, Guy's Hospital acquired one of the sturdy stone shelters and placed it next to an outer wall as a place for psychiatric patients to sit. It became known as the »lunatick chair«. Two more niches survive in Victoria Park in Hackney.

The first London Bridge was built in Roman times close to the present bridge and possibly repaired during the Anglo-Saxon period. The Normans constructed a wooden bridge, and in 1176 Henry II commanded a new one to be built in stone. At its centre was a chapel dedicated to St Thomas Becket, who had been martyred on Henry's orders. A drawbridge could be raised to let tall ships pass through, and fortified gates guarded the north and south approaches. As a warning to enemies, traitors' heads were placed on spikes above the gates. The broad piers of the 19 bridge arches restricted the flow of river water so much that dangerous rapids were created, and the pent-up Thames upstream often froze over.

It is well worth taking a look around the grounds of the hospital that Thomas Guy founded in 1721. However, to see the immediate successor to Old London Bridge, you have to go to Lake Havasu City in Arizona, where it was re-erected in 1971.

Address St Thomas Street, SE1 9RT | **Transport** London Bridge (Jubilee, Northern Line) | **Tip** In the attic of St Thomas's Church opposite Guy's Hospital, the Old Operating Theatre has been preserved in its original 19th-century condition, along with an apothecary's shop, the Herb Garret (9a St Thomas Street, daily 10.30am–5pm)

59___Old St Pancras

Bones and legends by the railway tracks

Given its location next to the high-speed tracks to Paris, the cemetery park around Old St Pancras Church is unexpectedly atmospheric. Pancras is said to have been martyred in Rome in the year 303. According to one tradition, a church dedicated to him stood here in late Roman times, which would make Old St Pancras London's oldest Christian place of worship. Roman tiles were found in its walls, but they may have been taken from a military camp. A different story relates that holy relics of this saint were brought from Rome by the mission to convert the Anglo-Saxons in 597. A stone in the chancel has been tentatively dated to the early 7th century, but in its present form, the modest church is the result of restoration in Victorian times.

The cemetery next to the church evokes even more historical associations. Here lie the bones of the composer Johann Christian Bach, youngest son of the great Johann Sebastian, and Mary Wollstonecraft, the author and advocate of women's rights. Wollstonecraft's daughter Mary Shelley, who wrote the novel »Frankenstein«, met her husband, the poet Shelley, in this cemetery, and they planned their elopement at the mother's grave. The striking funeral monument designed by Sir John Soane for himself and his wife is said to have inspired the design of the K2 telephone box (see p. 100).

Perhaps the strangest sight at Old St Pancras is a 150-year-old ash, the »Hardy Tree«. Tombstones have been placed around its trunk like the spokes of a wheel. It commemorates people whose bones were disturbed and jumbled in the 1860s to make way for railway tracks and tunnels. The architect's apprentice who had the task of moving the graves was the later novelist Thomas Hardy, whose poem »The Levelled Churchyard« contains these lines: *We late-lamented, resting here, are mixed to human jam, and each to each exclaims in fear, »I know not which I am!«*

Address Pancras Road, NW1 1UL | **Transport** Mornington Crescent (Northern Line) | **Opening times** Daily until dusk | **Tip** Via the rear (eastern) entrance to the cemetery and Camley Street you can quickly reach the Regent's Canal, where a 30-minute walk westward leads to the market and food stalls at Camden Locks.

60__ Orbit

An observation tower on the Olympic site

The 2012 Olympic Games were planned on the principle that the biggest party ever held in London should not be followed by a hangover. In place of leaving decaying, unused stadiums, which were the legacy of mega-events in Athens, Beijing and South Africa, the intention was to transform industrial wasteland into a large park on the banks of the river Lee, business and entertainment districts and pleasant residential areas. The sports venues have now been partly dismantled, leaving a downsized aquatics centre, the velodrome and the main stadium, which will be converted into the ground of West Ham United FC in time for the 2016–17 football season. Up to 6800 homes in five new districts are to be built by 2030 – and in the middle of all this will stand an eye-catching visitor attraction, a sculpture 115 metres high that doubles as a viewing tower.

The tower, produced through a collaboration of the engineer Cecil Balmond and the artist Anish Kapoor, is officially called ArcelorMittal Orbit. The billionaire Lakshmi Mittal made a large contribution, including steel that his company produced with 60 per cent recycled content in accordance with the Olympic project's declared aim of sustainability. The structure looks like a white-knuckle looping ride, made of red tubular steel wrapped around a central support. Two viewing platforms at the top present a 30-kilometre panorama across the whole of London for up to 5000 visitors daily. They are encouraged to descend on the spiral stairway of 455 steps, rather than in the lifts, in order to appreciate the sculptural forms while they orbit downwards around the main pillar.

Critics have variously damned this »snake that swallowed a broomstick« and »vainglorious sub-industrial steel gigantism«, or praised its organic shape as »a network of bulging red arteries« and »a generous drunken party animal«. The popularity of Orbit as a viewpoint suggests that the party has successfully been held without a hangover.

Address South Plaza, Queen Elizabeth Olympic Park, E20 | **Transport** Stratford (Central, Jubilee Line, DLR) | **Opening times** Daily 10am–6pm | **Tip** The White Building, a »centre for art, technology and sustainability« with a canal-side café, opened in 2012 in Queen's Yard, a short walk north-west of the Olympic stadium.

61___ The OXO Tower
Architecture as advertising

When you leave the lift on the eighth floor and find yourself in the reception area of a posh restaurant, the magic words are »viewing terrace«: if you make it clear that you have not come for an expensive meal, the staff will point the way to a small space high above the south bank of the Thames, where everyone may enjoy a wonderful view free of charge. Boats pass below, and straight ahead, the London skyline is spread out for landmark-spotting: Charing Cross Station and Waterloo Bridge on the left, the British Telecom tower in the background, Somerset House directly opposite, to the right Blackfriars Bridge and St Paul's Cathedral, all mirrored in the sloping glass wall behind you. Most of the terrace is reserved for restaurant tables, but at certain times of day you can simply drink a cup of coffee here without breaking the bank.

The whole building has gastronomic origins. The brand name OXO for beef stock-cubes was invented in 1900 by Liebig's Extract of Meat Company, which was an official sponsor of the 1908 Olympic Games in London and gave the product to all competitors. During the First World War, OXO cubes were part of the emergency rations for all British soldiers. In 1928, the company built a cold store and production facilities on the Thames, to which meat was delivered directly from South America. The Art Deco building had a slender tower, but planning permission to attach neon advertising for OXO was refused. The architect's solution was a vertical arrangement of three windows on each side of the tower: the top one O-shaped, the middle one an X, at the bottom another O, and they are all lit up at night.

The OXO tower was renovated in the 1990s. The two lower storeys now accommodate design shops and galleries. Above these are apartments; at the top, the high-class restaurant. Just don't ask the chef whether he uses OXO cubes.

Address Barge House Street, SE1 9GY | Transport Southwark (Jubilee Line) | Opening times Mon–Thu 11am–11pm, Fri, Sat 11am–midnight, Sun noon–10.30pm | Tip For reasonably priced meals and galleries selling art and craftwork, go to Gabriel's Wharf immediately west of the OXO Tower.

62 Parliament Hill

The whole of London at your feet

Although the hill is not quite 100 metres high, the view is breathtaking. To the south-east you see the skyscrapers of the City and Docklands, St Paul's Cathedral and the glass prism of The Shard. Far away to the left is the Orbit viewing tower in the Olympic park, straight ahead lie Westminster and the London Eye.

Parliament Hill gained its name in the 17th-century civil war, when forces loyal to Parliament occupied it during their campaign against the Royalists. Sometimes called Kite Hill, as it is one of the best spots for Londoners to fly their kites, this elevation is the southern end of Hampstead Heath, a precious recreational area close to the inner city comprising 320 hectares of sandy high ground. Its woods and open grassland are a fine place for walking, playing frisbee and picnicking. 150 years ago Karl Marx liked to come here with his family on Sundays for lunch in the fresh air. Until the 1940s, farm animals kept the grass short. Since that time, some parts of the terrain have been kept as heathland, but the woods have been allowed to expand. The heath is famous for its ponds, which originated as reservoirs. They are a habitat for amphibians and kingfishers, but also famous places to swim in segregated ponds for men and women on the east side of the heath, and the mixed bathing pond on the west side.

Hampstead Heath and Parliament Hill are a healthy place, therefore, where active people come for exercise in a bracing breeze. Yet linger awhile, perhaps when the light is fading or clouds hang low, to sense the spirits of the past – the travellers who approached London at twilight, anxiously scanning the shadows and bushes on the lookout for highwaymen, or the thousands of Londoners who fled here in 1524 because astrologers had predicted a great flood. From Parliament Hill they looked down on the city in trepidation – and the rain stayed away.

Address South end of Hampstead Heath | Transport Hampstead Heath (Overground),
then take the road named Parliament Hill | Tip Kenwood House to the north of Hampstead
Heath is a stately home with magnificent interiors by Robert Adam dating from the 1760s,
a fine collection of paintings and a lovely park (house open daily, 10am–5pm).

63_ The Peace Pagoda

Shining gold in Battersea Park

The view from the north bank of the Thames near Albert Bridge across the water to Battersea Park holds a surprise: a pagoda with a golden Buddha. This is the Peace Pagoda that the Japanese Nipponzan Myohoji order donated to London in 1985. Inspired by a meeting with Gandhi in the early 1930s, the founder of the order, Nichidatsu Fujii, dedicated his life to the cause of peace. From 1947 his adherents began to erect pagodas all over the world. They now number more than 80, mostly in Asia, but also in San Francisco and Brisbane, Munich and Vienna, Birmingham and Milton Keynes. Each June the London pagoda is at the centre of a peace festival for all religions. Nipponzan Myohoji also converted a storehouse in the park to a small temple and dwelling for the monk Gyoro Nagase, who came to London in 1984 to look after the pagoda. He became a familiar sight in Battersea Park, as he walked across the lawns each morning at dawn in his saffron robe, praying and beating a drum.

The pagoda of concrete and wood is 33.5 metres high and has two wide-spreading roofs. The spire above them consists of seven rings with a gilded pinnacle. Steps lead up to the lower level of the pagoda base. On the second level, which is not accessible, four golden reliefs represent the life of Buddha: his birth on the south side, his enlightenment on the east side, his death on the west side. On the north side, facing the river, Buddha preaches.

The surroundings, a charming 19th-century landscaped park, could hardly be more English. Visitors to Battersea Park enjoy a riverside promenade, fountains and roses, a subtropical garden, sports facilities, an art gallery and a café. The large lake is home to a colony of herons with 30 nests. The paths are used by joggers, dog-walkers, mothers with prams and every kind of city-dweller in need of a little respite. Buddha watches over them all.

Address Battersea Park, SW11 4NJ | Transport Battersea Park or Queenstown Road (Overground); bus 44 from Victoria | Opening times Park: officially 8am to dusk, park gates open 6.30am–10.30 pm | Tip At weekends in the summer months and daily during school holidays rowboats and pedaloes are for hire on the lake, bikes from a hire station in the park.

64_The Peabody Estate in Whitecross Street

150 years of social housing projects

»Peabody Trust« can be seen on residential estates in many parts of London. It is a charity, founded in 1862 by George Peabody in response to a critical shortage of housing. At this time, journeys by public transport from the suburbs to places of work near the city centre such as the docks were too expensive for most workers. Overcrowding and disease in inner-city slums were the consequence.

Peabody had already made a fortune in America as a wholesaler when he came to London in 1827 and multiplied his wealth in the banking business. He later invested shrewdly in American railways and was an active philanthropist on both sides of the Atlantic who endowed his trust in London with half a million pounds, a truly enormous sum at that time. The Peabody Trust built accommodations with high ceilings and large windows to provide light and air, as well as wash-houses and water closets for hygiene, and let them for reasonable rents. The first estate was built in 1863 in Spitalfields. Within 25 years, the Peabody Trust constructed 5000 homes, including those in Whitecross Street in 1883. The architecture, though solidly handsome, is austere in a way that matches the past and present regulations for tenants – cycling and skateboarding, ball games and music are prohibited in the courtyards, which have just a smattering of greenery. Sober, clean and orderly have been the watchwords for 150 years.

Until the 1970s, two flats shared a wash-house and WC in Whitecross Street. Though small by modern standards, the rooms compare favourably with most council housing of the 1960s and 1970s. Today, the Peabody Trust administers 20,000 apartments in London. A statue behind the Royal Exchange has commemorated its founder since his death in 1869.

Address Whitecross Street, EC1Y 8JL | Transport Barbican (Circle, Hammersmith & City, Metropolitan Line) | Tip On Thursdays and Fridays, delicious street food adds an international touch to the otherwise basic market (Mon–Fri 10am–4pm) in Whitecross Street.

65__The Piccadilly Line

Design and architecture in the Tube

The Piccadilly Line is dark blue on the famous map of the London Underground, that much-admired work of art that makes a complex web of eleven lines with 260 stations so easy to grasp. Many of the buildings of the Tube and their interiors also have artistic value, and some stations are listed monuments.

In December 1906, the first section of the Piccadilly Line, from Hammersmith in the west to Finsbury Park in the north-east, went into operation. A young architect named Leslie Green was responsible for design matters. His station façades of glazed terracotta tiles in the colour of oxblood, round-arched windows on the upper floor and clearly emphasised cornices are still highly recognisable today. Inside the stations, varied geometric patterns of tiles – white and yellow in Covent Garden, dark green and cream in Gloucester Road – adorn the walls and also serve the purpose of signposting.

In the 1930s, when the line was extended both east and west, the work was entrusted to a second talented architect: Charles Holden, who had already renovated the circular station concourse beneath Piccadilly Circus in 1928, adding the cladding of travertine stone that remains there to this day. He made a study trip to Germany, the Netherlands and Scandinavia to learn about the new Modernist architecture. He then designed stations of simple beauty using a lot of brick and glass, clear outlines, and contrasts between round and angular forms, for example Sudbury Town at the west end of the line and Southgate in the north.

For its 100th anniversary in 2006, the Piccadilly Line was brightened up by contemporary works of art commissioned under the common theme of »the travels of Marco Polo«, and the remaining original tiles were restored in Russell Square and Covent Garden. All of which gives even the most crowded, hot and stuffy Tube journey a certain aesthetic charm.

Address Between Heathrow Airport in the west and Cockfosters in the north | Opening times In central London, the Piccadilly Line runs from approx. 5am to 0.30am. | Tip The excellent Museum of London Transport sheds light on the technology and many other aspects of the Tube – including such design highlights as historic posters (Piazza of Covent Garden, Sat–Thu 10am–6pm, Fri 11am–6pm).

66__Pimlico Road Farmers' Market

Mozart and the magic fruit

At the border of aristocratic Belgravia with Chelsea and Pimlico, the junction of Ebury Street and Pimlico Road forms a little triangular space. Here stands a graceful statue of the young Wolfgang Amadeus Mozart, who composed his first two symphonies in 1764 at the age of nine while living at 180 Ebury Street. As the spot was not built up in those days, Mozart probably had a view of grazing animals and vegetable patches. Nowadays he looks down from his plinth each Saturday on carrots, apples and cabbages when local producers set up their stalls for the farmers' market.

Like other farmers' markets, the scattering of stands on Orange Square displays products that have not travelled any long distance. The aims of offering high-quality foods of known provenance, supporting individual rather than mass-manufactured goods and allowing the customer to meet the producer personally, clearly appeal to the residents of this affluent part of London.

On the triangle of ground beneath Mozart's gaze – it has no official name, but is usually called Orange Square – they find a rich mix of vendors whose offerings go far beyond fruit, vegetables and meat from their own farms. The fish stall sells the catch of the day from a boat on the south coast. Other stands are piled high with fresh pasta and many kinds of pesto, home-baked cake and a great variety of bread, locally made but inspired by France, Italy and Germany. The range of cheese runs from goat's cheese to mature Cheddar and lesser-known products from artisan dairies. The market furnishes everything for a good dinner, which might start with oysters or East Anglian crab meat and be washed down healthily with single-variety pear juice from Kentish orchards. The flower stall provides table decoration.

Address Corner of Pimlico Road, Bourne Street and Ebury Street, SW1W 8NE | Transport Sloane Square (Circle, District Line) | Opening times Sat 9am–1pm | Tip A shopping tour in this district could take in Peter Jones department store on Sloane Square and the expensive temptations of King's Road. For information about 20 farmers' markets in London, see www.lfm.org.uk.

67__The Police Lookout on Trafalgar Square

Keeping an eye on demonstrations

The usual sight on Trafalgar Square is of tourists eating ice cream or climbing over the bronze lions to take photos. However, the square has a more serious side, and its layout reflects the anxieties of the establishment about the unruly British people. When it was built after 1840, the purpose of the fountains was to make it difficult for large crowds to assemble. The architect, John Nash, planned the square in the 1820s at the same time as the fine new boulevard Regent Street, which deliberately separated high society in the West End from the poor in Soho.

Despite the fountains, Trafalgar Square quickly became a destination for marches and rallies. When 2000 policemen used their truncheons against trade unionists in 1887, 200 people had to be treated in hospital and three died. At a demonstration one year earlier, the commanding police officer, wearing plain clothes, mingled with the 5000 demonstrators, lost contact to his men (and his wallet to a pickpocket) and was helpless to prevent windows from being smashed in the gentlemen's clubs along Pall Mall.

Better communication was needed. The answer was to construct an ugly police hut with a telephone. When this was renovated in the 1920s, opposition to the eyesore resulted in an ingenious solution. On the south side of the square, two massive granite pillars support lanterns. The eastern pillar was hollowed out, a door and look-out slits were fitted in the curved wall, and a phone was installed. Many protests were observed from this discreet hideaway, from the »Hunger March« in 1936 to anti-war demonstrations in the 1960s. For surveillance of recent events such as the riots against government cuts in 2011, more modern technology was available. The phone has been removed, and the tiny room is empty.

Address Trafalgar Square, WC2N 5DN | **Transport** Charing Cross (Bakerloo, Northern Line) | **Tip** Diners in the upmarket rooftop restaurant in the National Portrait Gallery get a view over the National Gallery to Trafalgar Square. For a cheaper meal, go to the café in the crypt of St Martin-in-the-Fields on the north-east corner of the square.

68_ Postman's Park

A memorial for unsung heroes

After a few days sightseeing in London, you can get tired of monuments. On all sides, military heroes and empire-builders look down with a firm gaze from their plinths, and kings who deserve to be forgotten are honoured with statues. For the democratically minded visitor, a small garden near St Paul's Cathedral makes a refreshing change from this.

The artist George Frederic Watts (1817–1904) had been campaigning for a monument to unknown heroes for 30 years before his plan was fulfilled in July 1900. The first proposal for a site, Hyde Park, was rejected, and finally a decision was made in favour of a small green space laid out in 1880 on the site of an old cemetery. It was called Postman's Park because workers from the nearby General Post Office liked to spend their lunchtime there.

Watts' »memorial to heroic self-sacrifice« is a modest shelter built onto a wall with space for 120 tiles in five rows. Hand-painted ceramic plaques tell the story of ordinary people who gave their lives for others. A worker in a sugar refinery suffered fatal burns searching for a colleague after a boiler explosion. A railwayman drowned in the River Lea while trying to save someone who had fallen in. A 17-year-old girl protected a child from a runaway horse but died of her own injuries. One hero prevented the suicide of a »lunatic woman« at Woolwich and was run over by a train. Another died of exhaustion after rescuing people from the ice on Highgate ponds.

The people commemorated on the first 13 plaques, the beautiful turquoise-coloured tiles in the middle row, were chosen by Watts himself and made by the great tile designer William de Morgan. In the 30 years after Watts' death, his widow added a further 40 plaques in blue lettering with floral decoration. The most recent dates from 2009, and two of the five rows are still empty. A relief in the first row honours Watts himself.

P·C·HAROLD FRANK RICKETTS
METROPOLITAN POLICE
DROWNED AT TEIGNMOUTH
WHILST TRYING TO RESCUE A BOY BATHING AND SEEN · TO BE IN DIFFICULTY
11 · SEPT · 1916

P·C·EDWARD
BROWN GRE
METROPOLITA
MANY LIVES WERE
DEVOTION TO D
TERRIBLE EXPLO
SILVERTOWN ·

ELIZABETH BOXALL
AGED 17 OF BETHNAL GREEN
WHO DIED OF INJURIES RECEIVED
IN TRYING TO SAVE
A CHILD
FROM A RUNAWAY HORSE
JUNE · 20 · 1888

HERBERT PETE
STATIONER'S
WHO WAS DROWN
IN ENDEAVOURI
A MAN FROM D
APRIL 2

FREDERICK ALFRED CROFT
INSPECTOR · AGED 31
SAVED A LUNATIC WOMAN
FROM SUICIDE AT WOOLWICH
ARSENAL STATION · BUT WAS
HIMSELF RUN OVER · BY THE TRAIN
JAN · 11 · 1878

HARRY
KILBVRN ·
DROWNED I
TO SAVE HIS
AFTER HE
JUST BEEN R

Address King Edward Street, EC1A 4EU | **Transport** St Paul's (Central Line) | **Opening times** Mon–Sun 8am–7pm or until dusk | **Tip** 100 metres away at the corner of Newgate Street, the site of a bombed-out church, Christchurch Newgate, has been transformed into a fragrant flower garden.

69__Primrose Hill

A free panoramic view

The effort of making the short but steep ascent of the 78-metre hill north of Regent's Park is rewarded by one of the finest views of London. Primrose Hill is also the name of one of the capital's most attractive residential districts with its own village atmosphere. Together, Regent's Park and Primrose Hill, an area of almost 200 hectares, were a hunting ground for Henry VIII in the 16th century, and now form one of the eight Royal Parks, ancient possessions of the Crown that are now open to all.

The great advantage of Primrose Hill is its closeness to the centre of London. Parliament Hill at the edge of Hampstead Heath is higher but further north, so many details are less clear. The conspicuous features of the skyline from Primrose Hill are the high-rises of the City, The Shard on the south bank of the Thames; further west, the London Eye and the British Telecom tower. At the foot of the hill, the aviaries and animal compounds of London Zoo can be seen. In snowy winters, Primrose Hill is the best slope close to inner London for sledging.

It is hardly surprising that the district bordering the hill to the north-east is a sought-after place to live. Those who walk the streets here with sharp eyes have a good chance of seeing faces known from the media. Past and current residents of Primrose Hill include politicians such as Boris Johnson and Ed Miliband, writers such as Martin Amis and Alan Bennett, celebrities such as Jamie Oliver and Kate Moss, and lots of actors – Daniel Craig, Simon Callow, Jude Law and Helena Bonham-Carter. Imposing Victorian houses stand between Regent's Park Road and Gloucester Avenue, where high-class cafés and pubs that serve good food are to be found. Alternatively, buy ingredients for a sumptuous picnic, lay out a rug on the grass on a balmy summer evening, and enjoy the view of London beneath the setting sun.

Address North of Prince Albert Road, NW1 | Transport Camden Town or Chalk Farm (Northern Line) | Tip The Primrose Bakery is renowned for colourful cupcakes and home-made biscuits. They are a favourite at posh birthday parties for children, and are also sold at Selfridges, Fortnum & Mason, and Liberty (69 Gloucester Avenue, Mon–Sat 8.30am–6pm, Sun 9.30am–6pm).

70__ The Princess Diana Memorial Fountain

Splashing around is tolerated

When the landscape artist Kathryn Gustafson presented her proposals for a fountain to commemorate Diana, Princess of Wales, she explained that the work was intended to symbolise Diana's life. And truly, the memorial is beautiful, child-friendly, expensive to maintain, and controversial.

The fountain was opened by the Queen in 2004 in the presence of Diana's ex-husband and her sons William and Harry. Installed on a gentle slope near the southern border of Hyde Park, it is not a fountain in the usual sense, but a double watercourse. From its source at the top, water flows in two directions to the bottom of a large oval, where the streams unite in a basin. The bed of the streams, made from Cornish granite, is between three and six metres wide and 210 metres long. Three bridges, small waterfalls and changes of gradient add variety. Grooves, hollows and curves in the channel make the water dance and play. It foams, gurgles and bubbles, splashes up through little jets and slowly comes to rest as it swirls around the lower basin.

Shortly after its opening, negative publicity muddied the waters. People slipped on the shiny granite, and one child suffered a head injury. In autumn, fallen leaves blocked the channels. The fountain was closed for remedial work, including roughening up the most slippery surfaces. These measures seem to have been successful. In warm weather, the fountain now delights London's children. Adults too roll up their trouser legs and wade gingerly through the channel. Officially, visitors to the park may sit on the edge and dangle their feet in the water, but not walk in the fountain. However, the security staff who are constantly present turn a blind eye while young and old enjoy themselves. Diana would surely have liked it.

Address In the south-west of Hyde Park | Transport Knightsbridge (Piccadilly Line) | Opening times Daily from 10am, April–Aug until 8pm, April and Sept until 7pm, March, Oct until 6pm, Nov–Feb until 4pm | Tip The Diana Memorial Playground, with a pirate ship for children and benches for their parents, is at the north-west corner of Kensington Gardens (daily from 10am, May–Aug until 7.45pm, April, Sept until 6.45pm, March, Oct until 5.45pm, Feb until 4.45pm, Nov–Jan until 3.45pm).

71 _ The Prospect of Whitby

A last drink for condemned pirates

The Prospect of Whitby is the very embodiment of the notion of a seamen's tavern: the pewter-topped bar is supported by wooden barrels, the posts that hold up the low ceiling were once ships' masts, the uneven stone slabs on the floor date from the 18th century, and the fireplace is black with soot. Diners seated in the Admiral's Cabin, which has the appearance of a salon in a battleship from Horatio Nelson's day, have a view of the river through lattice windows, while those who take their glasses into the beer garden to drink a pint beneath the willow tree look out on passing boats – and a gallows with a dangling noose.

The gallows, although not genuine, is a reminder of true stories. Almost 500 years ago, an inn called The Pelican stood on this site. It is reported that the adventurer Sir Hugh Willoughby spent his last evening ashore here in 1533 before sailing round the North Cape to look for the North-East Passage to China. With his entire crew, he froze to death on the Kola Peninsula. He was not the only man destined to die who took a last drink here by the Thames. Just a little way upstream – the exact spot is not known – was Execution Dock, where pirates were hanged.

Punishing crime on the high seas, for example mutiny and piracy, was the responsibility of the Admiralty, which however had no jurisdiction on land. The gallows was therefore set up in the river-close to the bank, but in a place where it stood in water even at low tide. Condemned men were taken there in a cart and given a quart of ale before they were strung up. The last to suffer this fate were two sailors who murdered their captain in 1830. Corpses were left on the gallows until the tide had covered their heads three times. In some exceptional cases such as that of the notorious pirate Captain Kidd in 1701, the body of the felon was displayed in a cage for years.

Address 57 Wapping Wall, E1W 3SH | **Transport** Wapping (East London Line) | **Opening times** Mon–Thu noon–11pm, Fri, Sat noon–midnight, Sun noon–10.30pm | **Tip** The Town of Ramsgate (62 Wapping High Street), which also has a pleasant riverside beer garden, is also an authentically old pub. Next to it, Wapping Old Stairs lead down to the shore of the Thames.

72__Quantum Cloud

Art beneath wide skies

London is densely built in spite of its extensive parks. In the City, skyscrapers stand close to the noisy streets, and in the West End, the pavements are constantly crowded. Yet if you long for wide skies and a distant horizon, solitude lies only 13 minutes from Westminster by Jubilee Line, at the tip of the Greenwich peninsula. The Thames is wider here than in the city centre. Gulls screech, waves slap on the embankment, and the ebbing tide reveals sandy beaches. No buildings block the view across the water.

A little distance from North Greenwich Pier, a sculpture rises 30 metres into the air: a »cloud«. At its centre, a human shape can be discerned. Conversations with a physicist inspired Antony Gormley to create this work. Much of his art is concerned with the relationship of the human body to space and matter. On the beach at Crosby north of Liverpool, he placed 100 iron casts of his own body, scattered across the sand to be covered as the tide comes in. In 2007, he installed 31 male figures on the roofs of buildings along the South Bank in London. His most famous work remains the huge Angel of the North in Gateshead. Gormley constructed »Quantum Cloud« from angular steel rods with the outline of a tetrahedron that cluster loosely around the human form in their midst. Their position around the body was determined by random generation.

This airy, diffuse shape contrasts with a massive presence behind the observer: the O2 arena, the former Millennium Dome. Things are happening in North Greenwich. For the Olympic Games in 2012, a new cable lift opened to take passengers across the river to the Royal Docks at a height of 90 metres. Housing is being built on a large scale on industrial wasteland. Solitude will be less easy to find in North Greenwich, but by the riverside the feeling of wide open space will remain. The Thames Path shows the way east to the estuary and the sea.

Address Bank of the Thames near North Greenwich Pier, SE10 London | Transport
North Greenwich (Jubilee Line) | Tip A few hundred metres west of »Quantum Cloud«,
also on the river, is a work of art called »Slice of Reality«: Richard Wilson cut a slice out of
the middle of a cargo ship and left it for the current and waves to do their work.

73__ Queen Square

A green place for parents, children and queens

Who is the queen of Queen Square? The statue cast from lead in the gardens at its centre was long thought to represent Queen Anne (reigned 1702–14). The square, laid out in 1716, was named after Anne, but the figure probably represents Charlotte of Mecklenburg-Strelitz (1744–1818), King George III's queen. Her interest in botany is commemorated in the name of an exotic bloom, the strelitzia. Although Charlotte and George did not meet each other until their wedding day, they had a happy marriage. She bore 15 children and he, in a radical break with royal tradition, never took a mistress. The physician who treated George III in his later years of mental illness lived on Queen Square. It was decided that the King should live in his doctor's house for a time, and Charlotte is said to have rented the cellar of the house at no. 1 as a store for her husband's favourite food. Today, this building is a pub called The Queen's Larder.

Whether Anne or Charlotte, the statue is magnificent. It depicts a person of dainty stature with a resolute expression and curly, shoulder-length hair, wearing a crown and an opulent dress with a plunging neckline, a floral pattern and tassels suspended from the girdle. Her outstretched right hand once held a sceptre. One more queen is honoured on the square. In 1977, for the silver jubilee of Elizabeth II, a basin of flowers was placed at the other end of the gardens. Slabs on the ground in front and behind bear verses by Philip Larkin and Ted Hughes.

A more recent work of art on Queen Square shows a mother with baby in the middle of the gardens, which have been open to the public since 1999. They are much visited by young patients and their parents from the nearby children's hospital in Great Ormond Street. The square with its rose beds and flowering shrubs gives them a quiet place to sit when times are difficult.

Address Bloomsbury, west of Russell Square, WC1N 3AQ | Transport Russell Square (Piccadilly Line) | Opening times Garden 7.30am until dusk | Tip The café in the Mary Ward Centre at the south end of Queen Square serves reasonably priced vegetarian dishes.

74__The Regent's Canal
Leisure and work on the water

It is not necessary to leave London in order to take a long traffic-free walk. The towpath of the Regent's Canal, which runs over eight miles from Paddington Station to the Thames, fits the bill. The contrasting scenes of nature and industry, leisure and work, which accompany this canal walk already characterised the waterway when it opened in 1816.

The Grand Union Canal transported goods from the Midlands to Paddington. From the canal basin there, the Regent's Canal curved eastward in a great arc to the docks on the Thames, passing around Regent's Park and the high-class residential district that was being built there. Fine ladies out for a stroll were shocked by the bargemen's foul language, and the canal traffic was even a hazard: in 1874 a boat laden with gunpowder exploded and destroyed a bridge at the north end of the park.

Today, this stretch of the canal presents an attractive sight. At the canal basin in Little Venice, colourful narrowboats rock gently at their moorings. Bicycles, firewood, and even miniature vegetable gardens on the boats' roofs give clues to the lifestyle of the individualists who live aboard. Tourist boats take the short trip through a green cutting, passing London Zoo on the way to the markets and locks at Camden Town.

The stretch of canal to the east of Camden locks shows the change from dilapidated industrial sites to expensive housing. Commercial traffic on the canal ceased in the late 1960s. Cycling commuters have now taken the place of barge horses on the towpath. In King's Place to the north of King's Cross Station, a new waterside cultural quarter has sprung up. Elsewhere, old warehouses have been converted into apartments, but traces of decay remain, and with them, the feeling that you are seeing London from its untidy back yard, until at Limehouse Basin the Thames is reached, and expensive motor yachts line the quayside.

Address Little Venice: Warwick Crescent, W2 6NE | **Transport** Paddington (Bakerloo, Circle, District, Hammersmith & City Line) | **Tip** The London Canal Museum (12–13 New Wharf Road, Tue–Sun 10am–4.30pm; Tube: King's Cross) tells the story of the canal in a former ice store.

75 Richmond-on-Thames

Where the river takes on a rural character

Of all the structures that span the Thames within the boundaries of London, Richmond Bridge, opened in 1777, is the oldest and, with its graceful stone arches, one of the most beautiful. It is a starting point for lovely riverside walks. Towards the city centre, the path goes through the historic Old Deer Park to the Royal Botanical Gardens in Kew. On sunny days, the area to the south of the bridge presents a carefree scene of children feeding ducks and swans. Cyclists and walkers find an array of attractive cafés and pubs with outdoor tables. Rowing boats can be hired, and river steamers take trippers upstream to Hampton Court Palace and downstream to Westminster.

Although this pleasant small-town atmosphere provides a fore-taste of the rural charms of the Thames valley further west and gives the impression of being a great distance from the sea, this is in fact still a tidal stretch of the river. The tide reaches Richmond about 45 minutes later than London Bridge and moves a few miles further upstream to Teddington – more than 50 river miles from the estuary.

For a famous view of the Thames valley, leave the riverside at Richmond and ascend Richmond Hill along the road of the same name. The purchasers of houses on this road have acquired a fine prospect from their upper windows and made a rock-solid investment. One of them is Pete Townshend of The Who, who bought The Wick (halfway up on the left) from Ronnie Wood of the Rolling Stones. The neighbouring Wick House was built in about 1770 for the painter Sir Joshua Reynolds, first president of the Royal Academy. Down to the right are the well-tended flower beds of Terrace Gardens, from where it is not far to the highest point on Richmond Hill. Reynolds and Turner painted the view towards Windsor, which is as impressive today as it was in their time: meadows, trees, and the shining silver Thames.

Address Richmond-on-Thames, TW9 | Transport Richmond (District Line) | Tip Tide Tables under the arches of Richmond Bridge with its outdoor terrace is a recommended café. Up the hill, The Roebuck (130 Richmond Hill) is a traditional pub with a great view from the beer garden.

76_ Richmond Palace
A good place to live and die

Today, there are plenty of good reasons to live in Richmond. For those who can afford to buy a house there, the location on the Thames and nearness to the wide open spaces of Richmond Park are strong arguments. Richmond has upmarket shopping streets, good restaurants with a view of the river, and some fine pubs. One of the most attractive residential areas is Richmond Green, a large expanse of grass used for sports, children's games and picnics. On the west side of the green lie the remains of a royal palace: kings too found Richmond a good place to reside, and could reach their palace in Westminster comfortably by boat.

Edward I and Edward II both spent time in a manor house on this site, which Edward III then extended. It was known in his day as the Palace of Sheen, and he died there in 1377. His successor Richard II tore down the building, as his beloved wife also died there, and Richard was overwhelmed with grief. In the 15th century, the palace was rebuilt twice. It was more magnificent than ever under Henry VII – who also drew his last breath there. One of his titles, Earl of Richmond, gave the palace and town their new name. Henry VIII preferred Hampton Court Palace and left the residence in Richmond to his divorced fourth wife, Anne of Cleves. 60 years later it was the scene of one last significant death: that of Queen Elizabeth I in 1603.

In the late 17th century much of the palace was demolished. What remains today is a brick-built gatehouse adorned with the coat of arms of Henry VII. In the leafy courtyard beyond, a house on the right-hand side named The Wardrobe survives from the palace. Tudor Place on Richmond Green occupies the side of the tennis court – tennis was a royal sport in Tudor times. The four grand brick houses next to it were built in 1724 to accommodate attendants of the queen, and are therefore called the Maids of Honour.

Address The Green, TW9 1LX | Transport Richmond (District Line) | Tip The Cricketers on Richmond Green, built in 1834 on the site of an older tavern, serves hearty pub food and offers a choice between English ales and continental beer.

77___Richmond Park
Grass and trees as far as the eye can see

It is hard to believe that you are in a city of eight million people. Patches of woodland alternate with open expanses of grass, which grows tall in summer. No buildings are in sight. Richmond Park was enclosed in the 1630s as a hunting ground for King Charles I. The royal herds of deer then roamed over an area of almost four square miles. Walls and gates surround the park to this day, preventing 650 red and fallow deer from invading the suburbs. Their insatiable nibbling of green shoots and leaves has created the open landscape, as no saplings can grow here unless they are protected. The boughs of the mature trees branch from the trunk 1.50 metres or more above the ground, out of reach of the deer. 1200 ancient trees, especially oaks, grow here – some of them older than the park itself. Careful forest husbandry has preserved a diverse biotope for birds and insects. Richmond Park harbours more than 1000 species of beetle, some of which need rotting timber rather than an over-managed habitat.

Human hands, too, have shaped the park. Around the ponds and skilfully created watercourses of Isabella Plantation in the south-west, magnolias and camellias bloom in early spring, rare azaleas and 50 different kinds of rhododendron from late April. From the western edge of Richmond Park there are wonderful views of the Thames valley, and even a prospect that is protected by statute of Parliament. King Henry's Mound is a small rise from which Henry VIII is said to have gazed on St Paul's Cathedral, waiting for a signal that his second wife, Anne Boleyn, had been executed so that he could marry Jane Seymour. Today, visitors can stand on the mound with innocent intentions and look through a gap in the hedges and trees, if the visibility is reasonably good, for a glimpse with the naked eye or the telescope that stands here of the dome of the cathedral, 10 miles away.

Address Richmond Park, TW10 | Transport Richmond (District Line), then bus no. 371 or 65 | Opening times 7am (in winter 7.30am) until dusk | Tip The café in Pembroke Lodge, on the north-west side of Richmond Park with a great view, is open daily from 9am until 5.30pm.

78 __ The Roman City Wall

Londinium has not quite disappeared

London's ancient defences are not conspicuous, although their position is still recognisable on the map in the names of streets such as London Wall and Houndsditch. You can walk around the City for a long time without noticing them, and then unexpectedly chance upon a high wall of rough stonework.

The first Roman trading post on the site that is now the City of London was not protected by a wall. This made it easier for the tribal queen Boudicca to burn Londinium to the ground in AD 60. The three-mile-long, six-metre-high Roman wall was probably not constructed until around the year 200. 85,000 tons of stone were transported from Kent for the purpose. Six city gates were the starting points for roads that led to all parts of the province of Britannia. Through periods of decay and rebuilding, most of the wall that encircled the Roman settlement stood for over 1500 years. In the Middle Ages a further gate was built. Towers, parapets and walkways were added, but the basis of the defences was still the Roman wall. The gates were rebuilt again and again, then demolished in 1760 in order to widen the roads.

In the south-east corner of the fortified area, where William the Conqueror built the Tower, an imposing stretch of the old wall still stands. The Roman stonework stands to a height of 4.40 metres here. The two metres at the top date from the Middle Ages. Originally, the rubble core of the wall was clad with smooth-faced masonry, interspersed with layers of red tiles for stability, but the good-looking stones of the outer shell were plundered and re-used elsewhere over the centuries, leaving the wall with its present rough appearance. In this spot by the Tower, a little garden with a statue of Emperor Trajan lends dignity to the remains. More stretches of wall, including bastions and a moat, can be seen in the Barbican and near the Museum of London.

Address Tower Hill, EC3N 4AB | Transport Tower Hill (Circle, District Line) | Tip Excellent exhibitions in the Museum of London bring Roman Londinium back to life (London Wall, daily 10am–6pm).

79__Royal Arcade

Connections to the palace are good for business

When »The Arcade« opened in 1879, linking Bond Street with Albemarle Street in the high-class district of Mayfair, the idea of putting a row of shops beneath a single roof was not new. Covered passageways like this had been built in Paris almost 100 years earlier, and the English weather was an excellent reason for copying the plan. London's oldest arcade is the beautiful, though now sadly neglected Royal Opera Arcade on Haymarket, which dates from 1816. Three years later Burlington Arcade appeared on Piccadilly at the south end of Mayfair.

When it was inaugurated, The Arcade was not yet entitled to call itself »royal«, despite the richness of its architecture. Its classical façades have elaborate plaster adornments. Shoppers who care to take their eyes off the luxury goods and look up are greeted by lightly clad goddesses and their attendants, mythological scenes representing Prosperity and Plenty. The decorative details are picked out in white, orange and apricot. The view along the interior of the arcade is a fine perspective of round arches. Heavy lamps hang beneath the glass roof, and the large shop windows are framed in dark polished wood.

A shirt maker who had the warrant to supply the court of Queen Victoria gained the epithet »royal« for the arcade. A royal florist and a supplier of heraldic stationery were also present. Today, the products sold here are as fine as ever. They range from the fragrances of an exclusive perfumery to made-to-measure shoes, works of art and silverware for high-society dinner tables. A holder of a royal warrant is still represented: the chocolatier Charbonnel et Walker, maker of a drinking chocolate that the Mayfair clientele pronounces to be divine. Does Buckingham Palace order chocolate truffles for guests of state and evenings around the television, or cocoa for a warming bedtime drink? That, of course, is confidential.

Address 28 Old Bond Street, W1S 4SL | **Transport** Green Park (Jubilee, Piccadilly, Victoria Line) | **Tip** Mayfair is not only about luxury consumption. The Handel House Museum (25 Brook Street, Tue–Sat 10am–6pm, Sun noon–6pm) was once the dwelling of the composer George Frideric Handel. 200 years later, Jimi Hendrix lived next door.

80__ Shad Thames

Sought-after homes in Charles Dickens' slum

The works of Charles Dickens contain powerful passages about life in the poor quarters of 19th-century London. The south bank of the Thames east of Tower Bridge (then not yet built) was known to the novelist from visits that he made in the company of the river police. In »Oliver Twist« he described the houses around St Saviour's Dock: »rooms so small, so filthy, so confined, that the air would seem to be too tainted even for the dirt and squalor which they shelter; wooden chambers thrusting themselves out above the mud and threatening to fall into it … every loathsome indication of filth, rot, and garbage.«

Since then the scene has changed twice. The homes in Shad Thames, a street that runs parallel to the river as far as St Saviour's Dock, are now apartments in converted warehouses and shiny new buildings with a river view. Many residents are employed in the financial sector and take a short trip across Tower Bridge to reach the office. Expensive bars and restaurants around Shad Thames help them to spend their money. In 1873, three years after the death of Dickens, huge warehouses for tea, coffee, spices and grain were built here. The last of them was closed in 1972, and redevelopment began in the 1980s. The walkways that criss-cross Shad Thames high above street level, once connecting storage spaces on either side of the road, are now the balconies of flats. The names of the residential blocks – Vanilla Court, Cayenne Court, Tea Trade Wharf – are reminders of the old use of the buildings.

At St Saviour's Dock too, where a subterranean river, the Neckinger, flows into the Thames, warehouses have become fashionable apartments. In 2008 a campaigning environmental group cleaned up the narrow waterway where Dickens staged the dramatic death of the villain Bill Sikes and his vicious bulldog, which expired pitifully in the stinking slime.

Address South bank of the Thames east of Tower Bridge, SE1 2YD | **Transport** Tower Hill (Circle, District Line) | **Tip** The Design Museum (daily 10am–5.45pm) is to move from Shad Thames to Kensington in 2016, but the Fashion and Textile Museum founded by Zandra Rhodes will stay in the area: 83 Bermondsey Street, Tue–Sat 11am–6pm, Sun 11am–5pm.

81 __ Shadwell Basin
The transformation of a dock

The dock is a peaceful sight today: an empty expanse of water, connected to the Thames by a lock at its eastern end and surrounded by four- and five-storey housing from the 1980s whose round arches and covered walks are a nod to the style of the warehouses that once stood here. The basin was constructed as the eastern section of London Docks, facilities for loading and unloading ships within a walled area of twelve hectares. The calm water of Shadwell Basin is now the playground of anglers, dinghy sailors and kayakers. It takes an effort of imagination to picture the busy scene here 100 years ago.

Day labourers, unruly men without a steady income, crowded round the foremen early every morning in the hope of getting work. Ships from all parts of the British Empire unloaded goods here, especially luxury supplies such as spices, cocoa, coffee, ivory and hides. Visitors reported with excitement about wares with a whiff of faraway places piled up on the quayside, exotically clad sailors from all corners of the earth, shouts in strange languages, the rattle and clang of chains and cranes.

The London Docks were already outdated in the 19th century. They were never connected to the railway network, and the entrances were too narrow for large steamships. The business of the port of London shifted eastwards. Destruction by bombing in the Second World War was not followed by a new period of prosperity in this part of the East End, and London Docks closed for ever in the 1960s. In the following decades, most of the harbour basins were filled to make space for new homes. There are some survivals from old times. Canals connect Shadwell Basin with Tobacco Dock, where a storehouse dating from 1812 survives. On Wapping Wall stands the hydraulic plant that was used from 1890 to power cranes, lock gates and the two bridges that still span the entrances to the dock.

Address North of Wapping Wall, E1W 3SG | Transport Shadwell (DLR) | Tip The
excellent Museum of Docklands on West India Quay tells the story of the London docks
and dockland people (Mon–Sun 10am–6pm).

82__ Shoreditch Street Art
Legal or illegal, subversive or sponsored

The transformation of Shoreditch from run-down to hip began in the 1980s, when artists set up studios in vacant commercial properties. Cool bars and nightclubs followed in their wake, and start-ups from the IT sector clustered around Old Street. As rents rose in the new millennium, many artists moved further east, and in recent years, sleek new buildings have appeared. For the time being, Shoreditch remains a zone of transition between the City and points east, a place of galleries, unconventional designer shops and creative street art.

To the east of Shoreditch High Street, artists from all over the world have made their mark on walls and doors. On some streets, almost every available space has been pasted, painted freehand, sprayed using templates or adorned with little sculptures. Internationally known street artists have worked here: Banksy inevitably, Space Invader and Roa, who paints outsized animals – in Shoreditch a bird four storeys high. Some operate with the permission of the house owners, others illegally. Some studied at art school, others emerged self-taught from the graffiti scene. Some are sponsored by galleries that use attention-grabbing street art as publicity for their exhibitions, others oppose the art business on principle. One sprayer receives a lucrative commission, another is summoned for a court appearance.

Street art is a wildly creative cosmos of humorous, political or poetic work that is constantly renewed. Some works are quickly ruined by tags and low-grade graffiti, then painted over within a few weeks. The painting on the right, juxtaposing a British ultra-nationalist with a Muslim preacher of hate, has already disappeared. Work by respected artists may stay untouched for a long time, or even be repaired by supporters if it is defaced. And when all of Shoreditch becomes chic, street art will enliven another part of London.

Address Between Shoreditch High Street and Brick Lane, E1 | **Transport** Liverpool Street (Central, Circle, Hammersmith & City, Metropolitan Line) | **Tip** Not hip, but never out of fashion: excellent traditional fish & chips at Poppies, 6–8 Hanbury St., Mon–Thu 11am–11pm, Fri–Sat 11am–11.30pm, Sun 11–10.30pm.

83 __ Shri Swaminarayan Mandir

A Hindu temple, open to everyone

In Neasden, of all places, often mocked as the epitome of a faceless suburb and described by Sir John Betjeman as the »home of the gnome and the average citizen«, a gleaming white apparition rises above the rows of semi-detached houses as if transplanted from a fairy tale. A Hindu spiritual organisation, the Swaminarayan group, found cheap building land here – but otherwise spared no expense. Over a three-year period up to 1995, volunteers under expert supervision built a 60-metre long temple with domes and sugarloaf towers using Bulgarian limestone and 1200 tons of Carrara marble. The architecture is based on a Vedic texts and used no structual steel. The stone was carved in India by 1400 sculptors trained in depicting the world of Hindu gods, then shipped to London.

The result is breathtaking. Almost every surface is elaborately carved with swirling, snaking patterns and adorned by deities. Visitors arriving at the main entrance are greeted by dancers waving their stone limbs between deeply incised columns. The interior is almost more sumptuous than the outside. From lobbies whose ceilings are covered in wood carvings, the stairway leads up to the Great Hall, where an »arti« ceremony is performed every day at 11.45 am in a brightly illuminated space under a dome supported by marble columns and adorned with depictions of the Hindu gods.

Those who attend are expected to take off their shoes and dress modestly. Non-Hindus are welcomed sincerely to the ceremony, in which monks perform movements with burning candles in their hands in front of gaudily dressed images of gods to the sound of drums and bells. When this ends, worshippers put their hands to the candles and spread the divine power of the flame over their heads. After the ceremony, visitors can walk out onto a balcony for a close-up view of the temple sculptures and view an exhibition about Hinduism. It is an uplifting experience in an unexpected location.

Address 105–119 Brentfield Road, Neasden, NW10 8LD | Transport Stonebridge Park
(Bakerloo Line), then 15 minutes' walk (signposted) | Opening times Mon–Sun 9am–6pm,
for times of ceremonies see http://londonmandir.baps.org | Tip Next to the car park opposite
the temple, the Shayona Restaurant serves excellent vegetarian Indian meals at very reasonable prices (daily 11.30am–10pm).

84__ Soho Square

King Charles, Paul McCartney and Casanova

Soho has a certain reputation: a den of iniquity, full of striptease bars and the watering holes of drunken writers. A creative playground for musicians, journalists and the film industry, it might be added. The streets were laid out in the 1670s as an upper-class residential area, but soon high society moved to Mayfair, and Soho began its downward slide. Soho Square reflects its eventful history.

A severely weathered statue of Charles II in the gardens at the centre is a reminder of the original name, »King Square«. In its south-east corner, an impression of the early buildings is given by the House of St Barnabas, whose superb interiors, private garden and chapel belong to a charity for the homeless – the old metal pipe into which passers-by inserted a penny is still in place. In the 18th and 19th centuries, Soho had a sizeable French population, initially Huguenot traders and artisans, later aristocrats who had fled from revolutionary turmoil after 1789. The French Protestant church in the north-west corner of the square preserves this tradition. Another immigrant group, the Irish, are associated with the Roman Catholic Church of St Patrick, with its splendid marble and gilding, on the east side. The church occupies the site of a mansion where a celebrated Venetian singer and courtesan once received her lover Casanova. With holy mass held in Spanish and Cantonese, the church still cares for the souls of immigrants.

No. 1 Soho Square testifies to the creative side of Soho. Discreetly signed MPL Communications, it is the headquarters of Sir Paul McCartney's company, and has a replica of the old EMI studio in Abbey Road in the basement.

To take a rest and muse on the colourful past of this place, sit in the gardens. A bench is dedicated to Kirsty MacColl and her song about this place: »Your name froze on the winter air, an empty bench in Soho Square«.

Address Soho Square, south of Oxford Street, west of Charing Cross Road, W1D 4NQ | Transport Tottenham Court Road (Central, Northern Line) | Tip The Dog and Duck at the corner of Bateman Street and Frith Street has good beer, a cosy atmosphere and decor of the 1890s.

85 __ Somerset House

From government offices to a palace for the arts

»Shameful!«, said educated men who had travelled abroad. Foreign cities had imposing public buildings, but London was an unassuming clutter. A plan was made to build an edifice worthy of important offices and institutions. For this purpose, the court architect Sir William Chambers regretfully demolished a historic but dilapidated palace in 1775: the first Somerset House, built 200 years earlier for the guardian of the young King Edward VI and later the residence of princesses and queens, where the body of Oliver Cromwell lay in state in 1658.

Chambers' new building on the Thames adhered to the rules of classical architecture, as it was to accommodate the Royal Academy, the Royal Society and the Society of Antiquaries, in which the most prominent artists, scientists and historians of the kingdom were organised. Under their critical gaze, he designed architecture that was more for the intellect than the heart. In addition to learned societies, part of the Navy Office occupied the new Somerset House, which therefore had a watergate allowing access from the river.

To the first part of the building, completed in 1801, east and west wings had been added by 1856. For decades, this huge complex housed the Inland Revenue and the Registry Office: »No fewer than 1600 officials are employed, with salaries amounting in the aggregate to 350,000 pounds«, as the 1905 Baedeker guide meticulously noted. The last of them moved out in 2009. Somerset House is now home to the Courtauld Gallery with its exquisite collection of French Impressionists and post-Impressionists Works, temporary exhibitions, and the London Fashion Week. The great courtyard, once a car park for civil servants, is now open for all kinds of entertainment, from mid-November until early January for ice skating, and in summer for concerts. 55 fountains set into the paving delight young visitors by sending jets of water high into the air.

Address Corner of The Strand and Lancaster Place, WC2R1LA | Transport Temple (Circle, District Line) | Opening times Courtyard Mon–Sun 7.30am–11pm, Courtauld Gallery Mon–Sun 10am–6pm | Tip Simpsons-in-the-Strand, an expensive restaurant with an imposing interior, has been famous for its roast beef since 1828 (100 Strand, tel. 020/78369112).

86__ Spencer House
Old money, expensive taste

»Historic property in prime location, eight reception rooms (some renovation required), view of Green Park«. The agent's ad was not needed when the eighth Earl Spencer let his house near Buckingham Palace to Lord Jacob Rothschild's investment company in 1985 on a 120-year lease. The Spencers had not lived in their townhouse since 1926. In 1942, as a precaution against bombing, the furniture and many fittings were removed to their country seat. More than four decades later, Rothschild's company commenced an exemplary and breathtakingly expensive restoration of the building, which had been used for offices.

Spencer House was built from 1756 for the first earl by John Vardy in the Palladian style. The magnificence of Vardy's interiors on the ground floor increases on a circuit from the library and the dining room with its view of the park to the exuberantly decorated Palm Room, where gilded columns in the shape of palm trees frame a domed space in which a copy of the Venus de' Medici is the centrepiece. The highlight of the first floor, designed by James »Athenian« Stuart according to ancient Roman models, is the Painted Room, with frescoes on the theme of love for the happily married young earl.

During restoration work, copies were made of the original carved door cases and skirting boards, as well as six superb marble fireplaces (at 10,000 man-hours each), and 40,000 pieces of gold leaf made the Palm Room gleam again. With the help of loans such as paintings from the Royal Collection and furniture from the V & A Museum, interiors as sumptuous as any in London regained their original appearance. At the insistence of the lenders, the house is open to the public on some Sundays. On other days of the week, London's most exclusive event location is rented out at dizzying prices – during the Olympic Games in 2012 to the International Olympic Committee.

Address 27 St James's Place, SW1A 1NR | Transport Green Park (Jubilee, Piccadilly, Victoria Line) | Opening times Sun from 10.30am, last tour 4.45pm except Jan und Aug | Tip The daughter of the eighth Earl Spencer was Diana, Princess of Wales. The home of her parents-in-law is open to visitors in August and September: Buckingham Palace, daily from 9.30am, last admission 5.15pm (Aug), 4.15pm (Sept).

87 St Anne's Church, Soho

Where the German king of Corsica is buried

From Wardour Street, steps lead up to a garden by the tower of St Anne's Church. This former cemetery is a good two metres above road level, raised by the mortal remains of 60,000 people who were buried here in the 150 years before it closed in 1853 – 60,000 life stories, surely none of them more curious than that of Theodor von Neuhoff.

Born to a noble Westphalian family in 1694, Neuhoff was an agent for the kings of Spain and Sweden. He made a fortune in Paris through financial speculation, but had to flee from the city twice after running up gambling debts, and in 1736 became the leader of Corsican separatists who wanted to liberate their island from Genoese rule. They elected him their king, but the plan to invade Corsica failed. After further adventures, Neuhoff ended up in a debtors' prison in London, allegedly gained his release by pledging the kingdom to his creditors, then subsisted until his death in 1756 on the charity of prominent persons. One of them, Horace Walpole, composed the lines that can still be read on the tower of St Anne's:

The grave, great teacher, to a level brings
Heroes and beggars, galley slaves and kings.
But Theodore this moral learned ere dead:
Fate poured its lessons on his living head,
Bestowed a kingdom, but denied him bread.

Bombs destroyed the church in September 1940. The top of the surviving tower is an oddity that an architectural historian described as »two crossed beer barrels«. On open days, visitors can climb up to see the bell, dating from the foundation of the church in 1686, and the clock mechanism. From premises on Dean Street, the parish of St Anne's does valuable work for drug addicts and the homeless. The old south entrance to the church on Shaftesbury Avenue is now a souvenir shop.

Address Wardour Street, near Shaftesbury Avenue, W1D 6HT | Transport Leicester Square (Piccadilly, Northern Line) | Opening times Garden Mon−Sun 8am until dusk | Tip Soho is a bittersweet area. Patisserie Valerie (44 Old Compton Street) has been contributing to its sweet side since 1926.

88__ St Bartholomew

The court jester's church, now a film set

St Bartholomew-the-Great bears the marks of its 900-year history. Rahere, a canon of St Paul's Cathedral who is reported to have once been a minstrel or fool at the court of King Henry I, founded an Augustinian priory in 1123 outside the city walls next to an open space called Smithfield, the site of knights' tournaments and a livestock market, where William Wallace was executed and Protestants were burned in the 16th century.

In its present form »St Barts« is a rare example in London of the Norman style of architecture, but only the east end of Rahere's church building remains. When the priory was dissolved in 1539, the nave was demolished and its ground used as a churchyard. One of the doorways from the west end of the church remains. With the addition of a half-timbered structure above the old entrance, it now serves as a gatehouse. The church was spared in the Great Fire of 1666. A thorough restoration in the 19th century removed cowsheds and workshops that had been added. One wing of the cloister is still intact as a reminder of Rahere's original purpose, and the founder's tomb inside the church shows him in the garb of the Augustinian order.

Tiers of round-headed arches and contrasts of light and shade give the interior a powerful impact. Light streams through the clear-glazed upper windows, and the aisles beneath are dark tunnels. After the Sunday service, clouds of incense rise through slanting rays of sunlight in this ancient, hallowed space. No wonder film directors love St Barts, and have made it the setting for scenes from »Four Weddings and a Funeral«, »Shakespeare in Love« and »Sherlock Holmes«. It is no surprise to learn that a ghost – a monk looking for a lost sandal – stalks the gloomy passages. At night, the smell of burning flesh is said to waft over from Smithfield, where heretics died at the stake.

Address Cloth Market, EC1A 9DS | Transport St Paul's (Central Line) | Opening times Mon–Fri 8.30am–5pm (Nov–Feb until 4pm), Sat 10.30am–4pm, Sun 8.30am–8pm | Tip Smithfield meat market is the only historic wholesale market still operating in the City. It is best to visit early in the morning, but at any time its architecture in wrought-iron and glass, built in 1868, is worth a look.

89___ St Bride's

Slender steeple, creepy crypt

The graceful tower of St Bride's Church is often said to have been the model for wedding cakes. A close look raises doubts about this. The tower and steeple, 71 metres high, consist of a square base, five octagonal storeys, and an obelisk at the top. Even if a baker succeeded in copying this slender, complex construction, the proportion of icing sugar would be far too high to make an edible cake.

St Bride's is one of the most admired works of Sir Christopher Wren. Its magnificent interior was reconstructed following damage by fire bombs which left only the outer walls and the tower standing in December 1940. Restoration, which renewed the masterly wood carving on the altar and choir stalls, gilded rosettes and marble floor, was supported by newspaper magnates, as St Bride's lies just off Fleet Street and has been associated with the press for 500 years. One of London's first printers, Wynkyn de Worde, worked next to the church in around 1500, and was buried in St Bride's.

Wren's church of 1675 had six predecessors. There is a tradition that the first of them was founded in the 6th century by the Irish St Bride herself. Before that, a Roman house occupied the site. In 1210, Parliament met in the church. The diarist Samuel Pepys was baptised here, and the poet Milton belonged to the parish. Traces of many periods can be seen in the crypt, where excavations revealed forgotten burial vaults, one packed to the roof with 300 skeletons, and another containing bones and skulls carefully arranged in a chequerboard pattern. Among the items in the exhibition below the church is a patented iron coffin that was designed to foil body snatchers.

Until 1832, public executions were the only legal source of bodies for dissection, so the requirements of the medical profession for experiments and teaching had to be met by a gruesome trade in stolen corpses.

Address Fleet Street, near Ludgate Circus, EC4Y 8AU | Transport Blackfriars (Circle, District Line) | Opening times Mon–Fri 9am–5pm, Sat various times, Sun 10am–6.30pm; guided tours: Tue 3pm | Tip An outstanding choir consisting of twelve professional singers can be heard during church services twice each Sunday (for the programme, see www.stbrides.com).

90_ St Helen's Bishopsgate

Christ's message in the financial district

Work in the banking business »can represent a challenge for Christians who want to live for Jesus«, says the website of the church without overstating the case. For Bible groups and midday talks, St Helen's Bishopsgate opens its doors to employees from the flashy high-rises of financial institutions that overshadow it. Externally, the church looks squat and modest, which makes the light-filled, spacious interior all the more surprising. St Helen's has two naves, as the church of a nunnery was added to the existing parish church in 1210. After the dissolution of the convent in 1538, the division between the two parts was removed to make a wide space whose brightness today is the result of IRA bombs that destroyed the dark Victorian stained glass in 1992 and 1993.

It is worth taking time to explore St Helen's, as it has been at the heart of a prosperous community for 800 years. In the Middle Ages, rich merchants, anxious to secure their salvation and the family reputation, embellished the church. A father of City finance lies in a sumptuous tomb in the north-east corner: Sir Thomas Gresham (1519–79), who founded the London Exchange. The Renaissance monument to Sir William Pickering, English ambassador to Spain († 1574), is even more imposing. Framed by iron railings and marble columns, he lies with hands folded in prayer, wearing armour on his chest, delicate wrist ruffs and a trunk hose that looks as if it had been pumped up.

As St Helen's is not only a piece of preserved heritage but a lively meeting place for Christians, workaday items stand among the ostentatious tombs in quirky contrast: plain plastic chairs, chequered tablecloths and coat stands on wheels. To prevent utilitarian fittings from spoiling the church more than necessary, the legally required notice »Fire Exit« has been painted on the carved wooden doors in beautiful golden lettering.

Address Great St Helen's, EC3A 6AT | Transport Liverpool Street (Central, Circle, Hammersmith & City, Metropolitan Line) | Opening times Mon–Fri 9.30am–12.30pm, usually also Mon, Wed, Fri afternoon | Tip Diners in the Duck and Waffle (110 Bishopsgate, tel. 020/36407310) look down on churches and banks from the 40th floor of the 202-metre Heron Tower. Given this location, the prices of the food are acceptable.

91 — St James's Square

An address for the privileged, a picnic spot for all

St James's is a high-class area today, but in the 1660s, when the first Earl of St Albans received permission from King Charles II to build a new square, its pretensions were even greater. 50 years after St James's Square was laid out, the townhouses of seven dukes and seven earls stood there. Blue plaques marking the houses of eminent people name three prime ministers who lived at no. 10 and next door at no. 12 a significant mathematician, Countess Lovelace, who was the daughter of Lord Byron. Several 18th-century houses with fine interiors have survived – no. 4, for example, once the home of Nancy Astor, who married into a super-rich dynasty of hotel and newspaper owners and became the first woman to sit in Parliament in 1919.

In the 19th century, St James's Square lost its leading status to newly-built Belgravia, and the character of the quarter changed. Banks and offices moved in, and gentlemen's clubs opened on the square. Two of them have remained: the Naval and Military Club at no. 4 (former members include Lawrence of Arabia, Rudyard Kipling and Ian Fleming) and the highly exclusive East India Club at no. 16. Since 1841, no. 14 has been home to the greatly respected London Library. This private lending library with stocks of over a million books and agreeable reading rooms was appreciated by Charles Darwin, Virginia Woolf, Sir Arthur Conan Doyle, and has been used by many modern writers. In no. 31 on the east side, General Eisenhower planned the invasion of Normandy in 1944.

On weekdays, when the privately owned garden at its centre is open to all, St James's Square seems anything but elitist. Seated on benches by a path that circles the equestrian statue of William III, office employees, tourists and construction workers unpack their sandwiches and take the plastic lids off their caffè latte, or lounge on the lawn beneath plane trees.

Address St James's Square, north of Pall Mall, SW1Y 4LG | **Transport** Piccadilly Circus (Bakerloo, Piccadilly Line) | **Opening times** Garden Mon–Fri 10am–4.30pm | **Tip** 5th View, a café and cocktail bar on the top floor of a huge Waterstone's bookshop (203 Piccadilly, Mon–Sat 9am–9.30pm, Sun noon–5pm), serves decent food at reasonable prices.

92 __ St John-at-Hampstead

A village church for famous people

Church Row is one of London's prettiest streets. This irregular row of red-brick houses with fanlights and lanterns over the front doors, wrought-iron railings and 18th-century sash windows looks like a village street. Indeed, it leads to a village cemetery, where the gravestones have gained green layers of ivy and moss over many generations. Weathered crosses lean at crazy angles. Yew trees and chestnuts with spreading boughs plunge the sloping paths into deep shade.

The spacious church does not share the dark mood of the surrounding churchyard. It was consecrated in 1747, with large windows and galleries to accommodate a growing congregation. The first church probably stood on this site 1000 years ago. The committed ladies of wealthy Hampstead ensure that St John's is decorated with luxuriant flower arrangements, which is only fitting for a place of such distinction: a memorial commemorates the poet who composed his great odes nearby, John Keats, and the family tomb of John Constable, who painted the clouds above Hampstead Heath, lies next to the churchyard wall.

Constable is not the only prominent person to have been buried in this churchyard. John Harrison, a carpenter and clockmaker whose invention of the marine chronometer solved the problem of determining the longitude of ships at sea, was laid to rest in a fine tomb in 1776. The 20th-century graves include those of Hugh Gaitskell, leader of the Labour Party from 1955 until his death in 1963, the popular philosopher C. E. M. Joad (1891–1953) and Eleanor Farjeon (1881–1965), who wrote children's literature and the song »Morning has Broken«. Church Row also has its share of famous names: no. 26 was the home of Lord Alfred Douglas, whose homosexual relationship with Oscar Wilde led to the author's ruin, while the novelist and early science-fiction writer H. G. Wells lived at no. 17.

Address Church Row, NW3 6UU | Transport Hampstead (Northern Line) | Tip Keats
House (Keats Grove, March–Oct Tue–Sun 1–5pm; Nov–Feb Fri–Sun 1–5pm) was the
home of the poet from 1818 to 1820.

93_ St John's Lodge Garden

A sequestered spot in Regent's Park

At the heart of one of London's largest parks, an enchanted garden with a surprisingly intimate character is hidden away. It originally belonged to St John's Lodge, which was built in 1819 as one of 50 houses that were intended to make Regent's Park the finest residential area in London. This was part of an ambitious project planned by John Nash, who laid out Regent Street at the same time. Nash built the grand terraces that still stand all around the park, with their views of the lake, trees and lawns, but only two of the planned 50 detached residences were completed.

After several changes of owner (it is now in the possession of the ruling family of Kuwait), St John's Lodge was bought in 1888 by the Marquis of Bute, who desired a garden »suitable for meditation«. The secluded garden created for him became part of the public park 40 years later. To find it, go to the north-eastern segment of the park's Inner Circle and look out for an inconspicuous gate, behind which a path leads to St John's Lodge Garden.

Accurately clipped hedges and densely growing shrubs divide the garden into a succession of separate spaces. In the summer months, the flower beds are full of luxuriant blooms in harmonious colour schemes – for the pink-to-purple spectrum, for example, roses are planted next to campanula, matching lupins and cranesbill. The geometric layout of the garden frames views of the Lodge. Bowers covered with climbing plants provide shade, elegant seats invite visitors to settle down for the afternoon with a good book and, just as the Marquis of Bute wished, works of art furnish food for contemplation. A sculpture on the round pond depicts the youth Hylas, whom water nymphs are pulling down into the depths. According to the Greek myth, Hylas never resurfaced – and this garden is a spot from which you will not want to re-emerge into the noise of London.

Address Inner Circle, Regent's Park, NW8 | **Transport** Regent's Park (Bakerloo Line) |
Opening times Mon–Sun 7am until dusk | **Tip** The Regent's Bar & Kitchen within the
Inner Circle adjoining the wonderful Queen Mary's Garden serves afternoon tea and light
meals (daily 8am–5pm).

94__ St Pancras Station

An engineering miracle based on beer barrels

Passengers arriving at St Pancras International on the Eurostar trains from Paris are greeted by a masterpiece of Victorian architecture, an aesthetic and engineering marvel. The golden age of railway construction was coming to an end in Britain when St Pancras Station was opened in 1868. The engineer William Henry Barlow was therefore able to benefit from the experience of many predecessors. Whereas trains steaming into the neighbouring King's Cross Station entered two parallel sheds with a width of 32 metres each, Barlow designed a roof with a single span of 74.8 metres, a new record that was only exceeded 20 years later. Barlow's innovative construction of 25 pointed arches of iron, braced by lateral girders hidden beneath the tracks, enabled him to build a single span without an extensive web of trusses below the main arches, which would have detracted from the clean lines of the roof.

To the north of the station lies the Regent's Canal, which the railway had to cross in a tunnel or on a bridge. As the gradient that a tunnel would have required presented problems for locomotives of that era, Barlow opted for a bridge, with the consequence that the tracks reached the station above street level. The space beneath them was used by the Midland Railway to store up to 100,000 beer barrels, as part of the company's business was to supply beer from Burton-on-Trent for London's insatiable thirst. The distance between the 800 cast-iron columns that support the tracks was a multiple of the size of a 36-gallon barrel. The roof arches are twice as far apart as the columns. Thus the breathtaking architectural space of St Pancras is based on the Burton beer barrel.

The renovation and alteration of the station for its reopening in 2007 restored the architecture to its old glory and allowed light to flood through the roof again. The beer store is now the arrivals hall.

Address Euston Road, N1C 4QL | Transport King's Cross-St Pancras (Circle, Hammer-smith & City, Metropolitan, Northern, Victoria Line) | Tip The station hotel at St Pancras, designed by George Gilbert Scott, is one of the very finest examples of Victorian architecture. The restaurant in the old ticket office gives an impression of its superb interiors.

95 — St Sepulchre Drinking Fountain

A campaign against beer and cholera

Confronted by the technical wonders at the Great Exhibition in 1851, »Punch« magazine commented that a glass of clean drinking water would be more useful than anything that was on show. In the previous 50 years, the population of London had more than doubled to 2.4 million. The old water supply from wells, streams and the polluted Thames had become hopelessly inadequate. In 1854, Dr John Snow identified contaminated drinking water as the cause of the devastating cholera epidemics. Moreover, the countless horses in the city and thousands of cattle that were driven to Smithfield Market every day also needed great quantities of water.

In 1859, Samuel Gurney, a member of Parliament, founded the Metropolitan Free Drinking Fountain Association and inaugurated its first fountain the same year. It stands by the iron fence of the church of St Sepulchre-without-Newgate. Soon 7000 people daily were using this fountain, which occupies its original site, although it was removed in 1867 when Holborn Viaduct was built and not returned until 1913. By 1870, the association was operating 140 water sources for the people of London, and had extended its activities to provide troughs for animals. The temperance movement, campaigning tirelessly against the evils of alcohol, supported this work: it was no coincidence that many fountains were built close to pubs.

Particularly elaborate fountains can still be seen in Victoria Park in Hackney and in Victoria Tower Gardens by the Thames directly south of the Houses of Parliament. And drinking fountains are not a purely historical theme, as shown recently by the erection of one with a cool design in granite and stainless steel in the east of Hyde Park. Visitors to the park are grateful for a free drink.

Address Corner of Holborn Viaduct and Giltspur Street, EC1A 2DQ | **Transport** St Paul's (Central Line) | **Tip** In the Viaduct Tavern on the corner opposite St Sepulchre, you can order a glass of water, but a thirsty author preferred a pint of Fuller's London Pride.

96 _ Temple Bar

Where mayors greeted monarchs

Temple Bar is an imposing entrance to Paternoster Square and an embellishment to the surroundings of St Paul's Cathedral, but its significance was greater in its original location near the Temple Church, on the road that connected royal Westminster and the City of London. At the west gate (»bar«) of the City, the lord mayor greeted kings and queens when they paid official visits to the City. In a ceremony that still takes place occasionally, the monarch asked for permission to pass through, and received the sword of state as a token of loyalty.

By the year 1300 at the latest, a wooden gate stood on the site. In 1672, it was replaced by a new one made of the best Portland limestone – the one that is now on Paternoster Square. The façades, possibly designed by Sir Christopher Wren, are adorned by statues of kings of the Stuart dynasty: James I and his queen, Anne of Denmark, Charles I and Charles II, shown in theatrical Baroque poses with swirling robes. After the deposition of the Stuart king James II, the heads of traitors who had plotted to restore this very dynasty were placed on spikes on top of the gate.

As the London traffic increased, Temple Bar became a hindrance and was taken down stone by stone in 1878. The plan to find a more suitable site met with no success, so the brewer Henry Meux was allowed to erect the gate in the grounds of his country house, Theobalds Park in Hertfordshire. It stayed there for over a century, but was never forgotten, not least because a monument crowned by a superb griffin marked and still marks its old location in the middle of the road at the place where Fleet Street meets The Strand. In 2004, the remodelling of Paternoster Square finally provided an opportunity to bring back the gate. Its weathered masonry was restored, some coats of arms newly carved, and Temple Bar once again fulfils its old function of an entrance.

Address Paternoster Square, EC4M 7DX | Transport St Paul's (Central Line) | Tip
Although some new bank towers are higher, the best way to see the City of London from
above is to climb the dome of St Paul's Cathedral (Mon–Sat from 9.30am, last admission
4.15pm).

97 __ Three Mills Island

Grinding grain with tidal power

A large area in the Lea valley between the Thames and the Olympic site was an ugly wasteland left behind by the chemical industry until a few years ago. Thanks to the cleaning-up and greening of the waterways here, an older industrial location, which is anything but ugly, has more pleasant surroundings.

Mills on the place now called Three Mills Island were recorded in Domesday Book in 1086. They probably used tide power even at this early date. Rising water flowed into a reservoir and was retained there by sluice gates. It then flowed back into the river during ebb tide, turning water wheels. As this technology was perfected over centuries, by 1938 the mill wheels could be operated for seven or eight hours during each tide. In the 16th century the components of gunpowder were being milled here, as well as flour. Huge demand for gin in the 18th century kept the wheels turning to grind the required grain. In 1776 the Huguenot Daniel Bisson rebuilt House Mill in its present form, and 40 years later Clock Mill was added. The latter still has its clock turret and distinctive roofs above the drying floors. The grain was used to distil alcohol on site. Clock Mill operated until 1952 and is now part of London's largest film and TV studios.

In House Mill, possibly the world's largest tidal mill, water wheels with a diameter of six metres drove 14 pairs of millstones in 1880. Production ceased in 1941, but the River Lea Tidal Mill Trust is restoring the remaining four wheels and machinery with the aim of generating electricity. Visitors can admire the wonderful brick architecture of the mill and adjacent miller's house, which houses a café and education centre, and follow the processes from delivery of grain by boat to sacks of flour ready for collection. This is an industrial monument of the first rank, with a history reaching back more than 900 years.

Address Three Mills Island, E3 3DU | Transport Bromley-by-Bow (District, Hammersmith & City Line) | Opening times House Mill May–Oct Sun 11am–4pm | Tip Waterside paths lead north to the Olympic site and the park that is being created on the river Lea, or south to the Thames. For routes see www.visitleevalley.org.uk.

98_Tower Bridge Wharf
A clear view of the river

Walking east along St Katharine's Way, you see a round building on the right-hand side shortly before reaching Wapping High Street. Pass through the gate to see an open paved area with seats on the banks of the river. Here you can gain a different impression of the Thames than in Westminster, as it changes from an embanked and bridged city river hemmed in by large buildings to a major commercial waterway on course for the sea. Here the Thames gradually becomes wider, and the rise and fall of tides is more noticeable. Passenger boats passing at speed and the currents of tide and river send waves slapping against the quay. Wind ruffles the choppy water and makes it sparkle in the sunshine. This spot, Tower Bridge Wharf, is a fine place to linger, whether the sky reflected in the Thames is blue or grey, thanks to a wonderful view along the water and across to the south bank.

Directly opposite lies Butler's Wharf, where the largest tea warehouse in the world has been converted to luxury flats. Further to the right, the architectural jumble of new and old is almost startling: the brutal 1970s concrete tower of Guy's Hospital, the tilted egg-shape of City Hall and the piercingly self-promotional Shard line up one behind the other next to the Gothic silhouette of Tower Bridge. Turning to look along the north bank, you can see The Monument and St Paul's Cathedral with the British Telecom tower in the background.

After a rest at Tower Bridge Wharf, follow the Thames Path east through the redeveloped Docklands. A short way downstream, brightly coloured pennants flutter on traditional river barges. They are moored in front of new waterfront housing, past which the path leads to the Hermitage Riverside Memorial Garden. Here, in an area that suffered heavy bombing, flower beds and sculptures commemorate the civilians who died in the Second World War.

Address St Katherine's Way, E1W 1UR | Transport Tower Hill (Circle, District Line) |
Opening times Mon–Sun 8am–11pm | Tip The Dickens Inn at St Katharine Docks is
a tourist magnet, but good beer in a historic timber building makes it worth stopping there
(Mon–Sat 11am–11pm, Sun noon–10.30pm).

99 __ Trellick Tower
The rehabilitation of an architectural villain

Let's start with some straightforward facts. The Royal Borough of Kensington and Chelsea commissioned the Hungarian-born Ernö Goldfinger (1902–87) to design Trellick Tower. A separate tower for lifts and utilities is joined to the lobbies of the 98 metre-high main tower in the Brutalist Style on every third storey. After completion in 1972, 217 flats on 31 floors were rented to council tenants.

Goldfinger's character and work have not always been seen in sober, factual terms. As a student in Paris, he admired the Modernist architecture of Mies van der Rohe and Le Corbusier. In the 1930s, he married an English heiress, moved to London, and built himself a home in Willow Road in Hampstead that is now regarded as an icon of early Modernism in England and belongs to the National Trust. Its construction required the demolition of older houses. The author Ian Fleming, a neighbour, was incensed at this, and his dislike of the architect increased when a golf partner described Goldfinger as choleric and humourless. Thus Fleming found a title for the eighth James Bond novel and the name of his most infamous villain.

Trellick Tower was long regarded as a monstrosity, an example of disastrous housing causing social evils. In its first years, the building was notorious for drug dealing and violent crime. Changes for the better began in the 1980s through security measures and tenants' right to buy their council flats. Some privatised units in the block later changed hands at prices well in excess of 400,000 pounds. Today, glossing over problems such as the heat-leaking facade, estate agents praise »fashionable accommodation with an unimpeded view of London from the 30th floor (with lift and concierge)«. In the 1990s, the conservation authorities discovered the aesthetic merits of Brutalism, and sealed Goldfinger's rehabilitation by giving Trellick Tower a grade-two listing.

Address Golborne Road, W10 5NY | Transport Westbourne Park (Hammersmith & City Line) | Opening times By appointment. Search the internet for estate agents who have a flat in Trellick Tower on their books, and pretend to be a potential purchaser. | Tip Portobello Road, dreadfully overcrowded for the Saturday market, is a pleasant place to shop on weekdays. Golborne Road and the northern part of Ladbroke Grove with their antique and design shops are a mix of chic and shabby.

100__ Twinings Tea Shop
A pillar of the economy for 300 years

It is probably unique for a family to run a shop for 300 years on the same site. When Thomas Twining bought Tom's Coffee House on The Strand in 1706, tea-drinking was relatively new. Charles II's Portuguese bride introduced it in the 1660s, when the diarist Pepys recorded »I did send for a cup of tee (a China drink) of which I never had drank before«. The new beverage got a foothold in the established coffee houses. In 1717, Thomas Twining extended his coffee house, now called The Golden Lion, and soon sold more tea than coffee, much of it in the form of loose leaves for consumption off the premises.

During the 18th century, tea became popular, despite opposition. »The deleterious produce of China« supposedly harmed the health and weakened the work ethic of the lower classes. High duties were imposed and smuggling flourished, but tea became Britain's national drink, of course, and historians have recently claimed that the introduction of tea breaks during the Industrial Revolution increased output by refreshing the workers.

The Twining family sold fine blends to the upper classes. In 1787 they added the golden lion and figures of two Chinese that still adorn the doorway. In the 19th century the firm continued to prosper, and contested with Jacksons of Piccadilly the question of who first marketed Earl Grey tea. Today the long, narrow shop is a combination of retail outlet, museum, and tea parlour. Customers can brew a cup free of charge at the back – in homage to recent trends, green tea and fruit teas are also on offer – and view a little exhibition about company history, including porcelain cups, teapots, photos, and historic packaging. Twinings now belongs to a multinational food company, but a 10th-generation member of the family has a management role, and business continues under a logo that is claimed to be the world's oldest in continuous use.

Address 216 Strand, WC2R 1AP | Transport Temple (Circle, District Line) | Opening times Mon–Fri 9.30am–7.30pm, Sat 10am–5pm, Sun 10.30am–4.30pm | Tip The stunning interior of Lloyds Bank (222 Strand) with its painted tiles and decorative plasterwork dates from 1883, when it was a restaurant.

101 Tyburn Convent

A shrine to Roman Catholic martyrs

Near the roaring junction of Edgware Road and Bayswater Road is a place of tranquillity and meditation. It is no coincidence that the convent is here: the village of Tyburn, where Marble Arch now stands, was a site for executions from the Middle Ages until 1783. From 1571, the hangings took place on »Tyburn Tree«, a gallows in the form of a horizontal triangle with three supports, large enough for the execution of more than 20 people at the same time. An estimated 50,000 died here, surrounded by jeering crowds who expected them to be defiant and spirited in the face of death.

Not only criminals were hanged. Tyburn Convent commemorates 350 Roman Catholic martyrs. The first of them were sent to Tyburn for refusing to recognise Henry VIII as head of the Anglican church. After a brief pause under Henry's Catholic daughter Mary I (reigned 1553–58), persecution continued under Elizabeth I. Loyalty to Rome was seen as disobedience to the monarch and thus as treachery. The Catholics who died at Tyburn in the reigns of Elizabeth and her successors include two who were canonised: the Jesuit St Edmund Campion († 1581) and St Oliver Plunkett, Archbishop of Armagh († 1681, the last who died for his faith at Tyburn).

Martyrs' coats of arms line the walls of the plain chapel of Tyburn Convent, where nuns have lived according to the rule of St Benedict since 1901. They sing Mass seven times daily and keep silent vigil round the clock in adoration of the Blessed Sacrament, separated by a metal grille from the faithful who come in from the street to pray. Three times each day the nuns take visitors to the crypt, where relics such as bones, a fingernail and hair of the martyrs are kept. Outside the convent, traffic thunders along, the super-rich live in their mansions with a view of Hyde Park, and shoppers seek their consumer heaven on Oxford Street.

Address 8–12 Hyde Park Place, W22LJ | Transport Marble Arch (Central Line) | Opening times Mon–Sun 6.30am–8pm, tours of the shrine daily 10.30am, 3.30pm, 5.30pm | Tip It is worth taking a closer look at Marble Arch, even though many of the planned sculptures were left off to save costs. Originally the ceremonial entrance to Buckingham Palace, it was moved to its present site in 1851.

102__Waterloo Bridge
One of the best views along the Thames

A charming pop song of the 1960s, »Waterloo Sunset« by The Kinks, celebrates the beauty of the Thames. Two lovers meet at Waterloo Station and cross the bridge: »As long as I gaze on Waterloo sunset, I am in paradise«. In 1802, not far away on Westminster Bridge, William Wordsworth wrote that »Earth has not anything to show more fair«. The poet did not know that Waterloo Bridge would soon be built on an even more advantageous site, the mid-point of a bend in the river, which means that it gives passers-by a view of both Westminster to the south-west and the City of London to the east.

This first Waterloo Bridge, whose nine arches spanned the Thames from 1817, inspired painters and writers. It was a motif for John Constable and Claude Monet. A stage play named »Waterloo Bridge«, first performed in 1930 and filmed no less than three times, told the story of a soldier and a dancer who met on the bridge during a bombing raid in the First World War.

The second bridge, which still stands, was designed by Sir Giles Gilbert Scott and completed in 1942. The architect of the famous telephone box and two striking buildings on the banks of the Thames, the power stations in Bankside (now the Tate Modern) and Battersea, failed to create a beautiful bridge, but the panorama on both sides makes up for this. Close by are Somerset House (to the left on the north bank, when looking towards the City) and the National Theatre (on the south bank opposite). Further east St Paul's Cathedral, The Monument and St Bride's Church rise with the bank towers of the financial district beyond them and to the right. From the other side of the bridge, facing Westminster, the eyes rove past the cultural institutions of the Southbank Centre towards the London Eye and right to the unmistakable silhouette of Parliament. To stand on this bridge, beneath a wide sky and above a broad river, is to feel that London is truly a great city.

Address Waterloo Bridge | Transport Temple (Circle, District Line) | Tip You also get
a wonderful view from the two pedestrian river crossings on either side of the Hungerford
Railway Bridge, to the south of Waterloo Bridge.

103__Wellington Arch

A warrior and an angel of peace

A great deal was expected of the triumphal arch that was erected near the south-east corner of Hyde Park in 1827. It was intended to celebrate victory over Napoleon, to constitute the western gateway to London, and to mark a processional way to Buckingham Palace. The architect Decimus Burton produced correspondingly grand designs, but a costly palace extension for free-spending King George IV meant that the arch had to be simplified. Most of the sculptural decoration was omitted.

The arch stood on the south side of Piccadilly opposite the London residence of the Duke of Wellington, who defeated Napoleon at the Battle of Waterloo. In his honour, the largest equestrian statue ever made was placed on the new triumphal arch. Many commentators held this 8.5-metre-high colossus to be ridiculous, but it had to stay: the statue of the Duke stood practically on the doorstep of the man whom it represented, and to remove it would have been an insult.

When Piccadilly was widened in 1883, the arch was moved a few yards. This was the opportunity to take down the statue, as Wellington was no longer alive, but 30 years were to pass before the quadriga that now crowns the arch was completed. Its sculptor, Adrian Jones, created four high-spirited horses and a chariot onto which descends an angel of peace bearing an olive branch and laurel wreath. This dramatic work is the largest bronze sculpture in Europe.

Until the 1950s, Wellington Arch was London's smallest police station. Today its south half is used to ventilate the pedestrian subway under the surrounding roads. The other side of the arch houses an exhibition, including a photograph of Adrian Jones taking afternoon tea in the belly of one of the horses. The view from the roof across Hyde Park and down Constitution Hill to Buckingham Palace is best in winter, when the trees have lost their leaves.

Address Hyde Park Corner, W1J 7JZ | Transport Hyde Park Corner (Piccadilly Line) | Opening times Mon–Sun April–Sept 10am–6pm, Oct until 5pm, Nov–March until 4pm | Tip Ye Grapes (16 Shepherd Market, Mon–Sat 11am–11pm, Sun noon–10.30pm) is a cosy Victorian pub in an attractive corner of Mayfair.

104__The Westbourne

The stream that flows through a Tube station

Subterranean rivers are, needless to say, invisible. There is an exception to this in the Tube station at Sloane Square, where the Westbourne crosses the tracks above the heads of passengers waiting on the platforms. They hear no splashes and see no water, as the stream flows through a closed iron trough. Nevertheless, to look up at the black-painted underside of the aqueduct is a rare opportunity to glimpse one of the many watercourses that otherwise lie unseen beneath the city streets.

21 small rivers and streams flow into the Thames within the boundaries of Greater London. Some of them run through the suburbs above ground, but in the city centre, they all disappeared from view long ago. The Walbrook, for example, on whose banks the history of London began 2000 years ago, was covered up in the 1440s. The Tyburn passes beneath Buckingham Palace. The Fleet River, which rises on Hampstead Heath and enters the Thames near Blackfriars Bridge, was hidden underground in the 18th century, although the quays on its banks were commercially useful, because it gave off an intolerable stench.

The source of the Westbourne is on the west side of Hampstead Heath. It flows, already below the earth, through Kilburn and Maida Vale towards Paddington Station, where its course is parallel to Westbourne Terrace. From 1731 its waters fed a new lake in Hyde Park, The Serpentine, but became so polluted that in the 19th century they had to be diverted through a channel around the north side of the lake. After flowing beneath Belgravia, the Westbourne makes its brief appearance at Sloane Square Station, then continues below Holbein Place and the gardens of the Royal Hospital to its outlet near Chelsea Bridge. By looking from the bridge at low tide, it is possible to see the main outfall a short distance upstream, and two smaller ones on the opposite side.

Address Sloane Square | **Transport** Sloane Square (Circle, District Line) | **Tip** The Saatchi Gallery, a major influence on British contemporary art since 1985, found a new home in converted barracks near Sloane Square in 2008 (Duke of York's HQ, King's Road, daily 10am–6pm, free admission).

105 __ Westminster Cathedral

The Cinderella cathedral in search of finery

We are not talking about Westminster Abbey, that glorious setting for coronations and royal weddings. In comparison to the 950-year-old abbey, the cathedral of the same name is a poor relation, as it does not belong to the established Church of England but is a Roman Catholic place of worship where Mass has only been celebrated since 1903.

To meet the needs of the rapidly growing number of Catholics in Britain in the 19th century, the Vatican created a church hierarchy for the kingdom. The new archdiocese of Westminster laid the foundation stone for its cathedral in 1895 on the site of a demolished prison. In order to differentiate the building from the Gothic and classical styles characteristic of the Anglican church, the architect John Francis Bentley looked to Byzantine architecture. However, the interior decoration to match this style required a lot of mosaics and marble – and the financial means were not available. Although work has been continuing for decades, naked masonry is still visible on walls and vaults.

In fact, this imperfection lends visual appeal to the cathedral. Dark raw surfaces adjoin pillars clad in smooth, precious marble. Golden mosaics shine in the chapels, and the pulpit is covered in sumptuous cut stone of many colours, but a glance upwards reveals brickwork blackened by the soot from candles. The fine relief carvings of the Stations of the Cross were produced by Eric Gill after 1914. Much of the interior has been splendidly adorned with over 100 different kinds of marble, but the continuation of the work depends on the flow of donations. In contrast to the eye-wateringly expensive admission fee for St Paul's Cathedral and Westminster Abbey, Westminster Cathedral welcomes visitors without payment. With its red-and-white banded exterior and tall tower, this church is a beacon among the soulless modern glass façades on Victoria Street.

Address Victoria Street, SW1P 1QW | **Transport** Victoria (Circle, District, Victoria Line) | **Opening times** Cathedral Mon–Sun from 7am; tower, exhibition and treasury Mon–Fri 9.30am–5pm, Sat–Sun 9.30am–6pm | **Tip** The Albert (52 Victoria Street, Mon–Sun 12 noon–11pm), a pub dating from 1864 with an original interior, is appreciated by members of Parliament for its hearty food and good ales.

106 Whitechapel Bell Foundry

Where Big Ben was cast

In 2012, one of the most remarkable companies in London was working flat out. Whitechapel Bell Foundry had received orders from churches all over the country to commemorate the diamond jubilee of Elizabeth II, and was responsible for designing and tuning (though not casting) the 23-ton bell that chimed during the opening ceremony of the Olympic Games in that year, the biggest commission in the company's history.

This history is something to be proud of. Founded in 1570, the Whitechapel Bell Foundry is the oldest continuously producing company in England. The first bell-founder who worked in Whitechapel, Robert Mot, made bells that still ring today. Two of them hang in the north-west tower of Westminster Abbey. In 1738, production moved to the present site, where famous bells have been cast. They include Big Ben (1858), at 13.8 tons then the largest bell ever made in Britain. It was carried to Parliament on a cart pulled by 16 beribboned horses across London Bridge, through Southwark and then over Westminster Bridge as crowds lined the streets. The Liberty Bell in Philadelphia (1752), a hallowed symbol of the independence of the United States, also came from Whitechapel.

Today, the fourth generation of the Hughes family runs the business. The offices and a small museum are on the ground floor of a house built in 1670. Visitors walk through a template showing the size of Big Ben into small exhibition rooms to see historic photos, details of bells that have been cast in Whitechapel, and a home-made model of the foundry to illustrate the stages in the production process. The popularity of church bells in Britain is cause to be optimistic that the company's future will be as long as its history. The inscription on the Olympic bell backs this up with a fitting quote from Shakespeare's »The Tempest«: »Be not afeard, the isle is full of noises«.

Address 32–34 Whitechapel Road, E1 1DY | Transport Aldgate East (District, Hammersmith & City Line) | Opening times Museum Mon–Fri 9am–5pm; for tours of the foundry, see www.whitechapelbellfoundry.co.uk | Tip A short walk from the foundry, Tayyabs (83 Fieldgate Street, tel. 020/72479543, reservation recommended, Mon–Sun noon–11.30pm) is known for its excellent Punjabi food.

107_Whitechapel Gallery
Art for all and a golden tree

When the Whitechapel Gallery opened in 1901, its founders' aim was to make culture, especially contemporary art, accessible to the poor of the East End. The façade of the gallery expressed this spirit of innovation and idealism thanks to its unusual asymmetrical design with Art Nouveau influence by Charles Harrison Townsend. The mosaic frieze that was planned for the recess between the two towers was never carried out, but the motif of the Tree of Life on terracotta panels on the lower parts of the towers symbolised growth, learning and renewal.

Since its early days, the gallery has taken a pioneering role. In 1938 it exhibited Picasso's »Guernica« in response to a nascent fascist movement that deliberately provoked the many Jewish and left-wing inhabitants of Whitechapel. In 1956, the exhibition »This Is Tomorrow« was the first in England to show Pop Art. Jackson Pollock, Mark Rothko and Frida Kahlo were first presented to the London art scene in this gallery, which also promoted British artists such as Gilbert & George. A well-known contemporary artist who has lived near Whitechapel Gallery for 25 years, Rachel Whiteread, has now remodelled its façade.

Much of Whiteread's work involves making casts of large and small objects, thus creating modern sculptures with historical references. She first came to prominence in 1993 with a full-size cast of the interior of a complete house in the East End. For the Whitechapel Gallery, she placed four casts of the existing windows between the towers, and added golden decoration derived from the terracotta Trees of Life: bronze replicas of their branches and leaves scattered across the recess and the towers. Whiteread thus refers to the history of the gallery, which was reopened in 2009 with twice as much exhibition space as before and continues to fulfil its original purpose of bringing art to east London.

Address 77–82 Whitechapel High Street, E1 7QX | Transport Aldgate East (District, Hammersmith & City Line) | Opening times Tue, Wed, Fri–Sun 11am–6pm, Thu 11am–9pm | Tip For the art programme First Thursdays, over 150 galleries and museums in East London open until 9pm on the first Thursday of the month. Most of the exhibitions, performances, concerts and guided tours are free (www.firstthursdays.co.uk).

108— The Wildflower Garden in Lambeth

Colour among the gravestones

At first sight, London's urban jungle may not seem like the ideal place to celebrate the history of gardening. Nevertheless, carefully tended front gardens in the suburbs, densely planted window boxes in the inner city and the flower beds in public parks keep the city in bloom from early spring to late autumn. In and around the church of St Mary-at-Lambeth, different faces of the English garden tradition are on view.

There was a good reason to set up the Museum of Garden History in this deconsecrated church, which was in such a ruinous condition in the early 1970s that it was almost demolished. In the churchyard is the tomb of two pioneering plant hunters and gardeners, John Tradescant the Elder (1570–1638) and the Younger (1608–62), both of them intrepid travellers. Around their grave grow plants that they introduced to Europe such as the scarlet runner bean and tulip tree. The garden behind the church belongs to the museum, but it is not necessary to pay the entrance fee in order to admire the colourful wild flower garden at the front, where a luxuriant growth of grasses and wild flowers among old graves creates a mood of morbid decay mixed with the freshness of spring. In April, forget-me-nots and cranesbill flower, followed by foxgloves, marguerites, marigolds and campions. In June, poppies bloom in many colours, and in late summer, hollyhocks rise above the gravestones. Two notable persons are buried here: Elias Ashmole, founder of the world's first university museum in Oxford, and Captain Bligh of The Bounty.

An untended patch of land just outside the churchyard also takes up the theme of nature in the city. A fountain is surrounded by mosaic pictures of motifs chosen by local children: a hedgehog, a fox, a peach and a butterfly.

Address Lambeth Palace Road, SE1 7LB | **Transport** Westminster (Circle, District, Jubilee Line) | **Opening times** Museum of Garden History Sun–Fri 10.30am–5pm, Sat 10.30am–4pm | **Tip** A few paces away is Lambeth Palace, the London seat of the archbishops of Canterbury. For tours of the palace, see www.ticketmaster.co.uk. For exhibitions in the historic library there, see www.lambethpalacelibrary.org.

109__Wilton's Music Hall

Bare boards, crumbling plaster

This small theatre has survived everything that fate could throw at it: a fire in 1877, the Blitz of 1940–41, slum clearances in the 1960s and decades of neglect. From the street, there is no sign of a theatre – only a row of terraced houses with traces of red paint on a shabby façade. The decay becomes clearer when you enter the hallway, where the floorboards are bare and the brick walls have lost their plaster. In the auditorium beyond, delicate spiral columns support the galleries. After a short time, as your eyes get used to the darkness, the remains of stucco decoration and gilding become visible. Welcome to Wilton's Music Hall, the last of its kind!

19th-century music-hall shows comprehended everything that could make the public laugh, cry or cheer: from singers and comedians to acrobats, ventriloquists, dancers and sword-swallowers. At Wilton's, this entertainment developed from sing-songs in a seamen's tavern in the 1740s. A concert hall built behind the pub in 1839 was enlarged 20 years later by John Wilton. He constructed a high stage to give the audience a clear view, even over the top hats of gentlemen who came from the West End to indulge in some low life, and adorned the room with mirrors, crystal chandeliers and a »sunlight« with 100 gas jets to make everything sparkle. Oscar Wilde's »Picture of Dorian Gray« describes how such a light »flamed like a monstrous dahlia with petals of yellow fire«.

The days of glory were soon over. Splendid new theatres supplanted simple halls like Wilton's, which became a Methodist mission and finally a storehouse. In 1971 it was listed as the only surviving first-generation music hall. Years of fund-raising and publicity work are now coming to fruition in restoration and careful modernisation which will make Wilton's fit for operation as a theatre without spoiling its morbid charm. Go there after dark and listen: does the laughter of past times still echo?

Address 1 Grace's Alley, Ensign Street, E1 8JB | Transport Tower Hill (Circle, District Line), Tower Gateway (DLR) | Opening times For events in the Mahogany Bar during restoration, or food and drink in the Green Room, see www.wiltons.org.uk | Tip A short trip by Tube from Wilton's takes you to many historic theatres, for example the Victoria Palace Theatre, built in 1911 for music hall entertainments near Victoria Station.

110__Ye Olde Mitre

A well-hidden pub

A pub that is so difficult to find, is closed on weekends, and yet has stayed in business for centuries, must have something special. To discover its secret, turn left from Holborn Circus into Hatton Garden and look out for a narrow passage by the fifth building on the right. Or pass through the gates at the end of Ely Place and turn left into the passage. In front of a façade of wood and bull's-eye window panes, the sign »Ye Olde Mitre« depicts a bishop's hat and names the year 1546, when a tavern first started to serve beer on the grounds of a bishop's palace.

The present building dates from 1773. Its furnishings of wooden panelling, bench seats around the walls, and spacious armchairs are a mere 80 years old, but convincingly create the atmosphere of an ancient tavern, especially after a pint or two: the Mitre is known for the good quality of its ales, which are drawn from hand pumps at the bar between two of the lounges. In the back room, water jugs hang from the ceiling and wall lights provide subdued illumination. The front room has a fireplace and a real historical curiosity: the trunk of a cherry tree that once marked the property boundary. According to tradition, Queen Elizabeth I danced around this tree with her court favourite, Sir Christopher Hatton. Whether this really happened or not, it is known that Elizabeth put pressure on the Bishop of Ely to sell part of the palace to Hatton, and liked to visit her courtier there.

The only remaining part of the palace is its chapel, St Etheldreda on Ely Place. The gates and guardhouse at the end of this private road are a reminder that it belonged to a closed precinct under the bishops' jurisdiction. The entrance to Ye Olde Mitre harks back to London's past, when the city was a warren of dark alleys and hidden courtyards. Good beer, filling pies, and loyal customers ensure that it will also be part of London's future.

Address 1 Ely Court, Ely Place, EC1N 6SJ | **Transport** Chancery Lane (Central Line) | **Opening times** Mon–Fri 11am–11pm | **Tip** St Etheldreda's (open Mon–Sat 8am–5pm, Sun 8am–12.30pm) on Ely Place was built in around 1290. It has been a Roman Catholic church since restoration in 1873, and gained new stained-glass windows in the 1950s following war damage.

112_ York Watergate

An imposing entrance is all that remains

Between the bustle of Villiers Street and the beauty of Victoria Embankment Gardens stands a relic from the days when the grand houses of noblemen lined The Strand. Behind them, gardens sloped down to the banks of the Thames, where each residence had its own boats moored at a pier, as it was much more comfortable to travel on the river than to jolt over badly paved streets in a coach. York Watergate was built in 1626 as the river entrance to York House for the Duke of Buckingham.

The handsome and elegant Buckingham was the chief minister – also, it was rumoured, the lover – of King James I. York House, which was the palace of the bishops of Norwich in the 13th century and later passed to the archbishops of York, was a convenient and fitting home, a short distance from his monarch's Whitehall Palace and close to the houses of other high-ranking aristocrats. Buckingham's son sold the estate to developers in 1672, but stipulated that the family name, at least, would remain: the streets to be built on the site were called, in accordance with his title »George Villiers, Duke of Buckingham«, Villiers Street and Buckingham Street (as they still are today); Duke Street and George Street (later renamed John Adam Street and York Buildings respectively); and, because the title needed its preposition, »Of Alley« (now the passageway York Place off Villiers Street).

York House was torn down, but the watergate stayed. Lions, shells and the arms of the Villiers family adorn its Thames façade, and the family motto is inscribed on the back. Construction of the Embankment left the gate stranded, 150 metres from the river, but 19th-century paintings depict it as it once looked. In scenes reminiscent of Venice, romantic by moonlight or festive for the procession of boats at Admiral Nelson's funeral, it stands on the riverbank with water lapping at its steps.

Address Watergate Walk, WC2N 6NE | Transport Embankment (Bakerloo, Circle, District, Northern Line) | Tip The famous Gordon's Wine Bar, unchanged for decades, has provided dark corners for discreet conversations since 1890 (47 Villiers Street, Mon–Sat 11am–11pm, Sun noon–10pm).

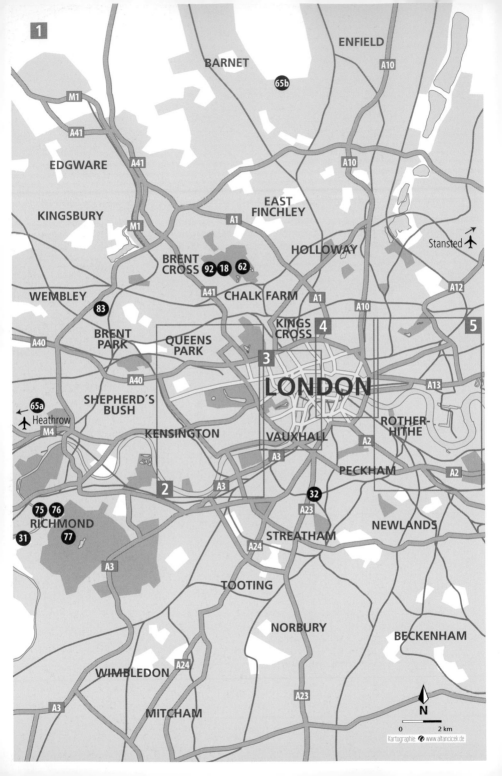

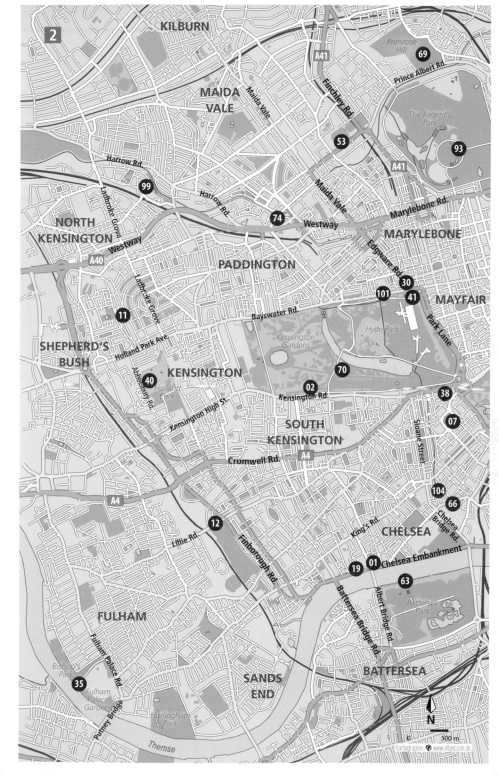

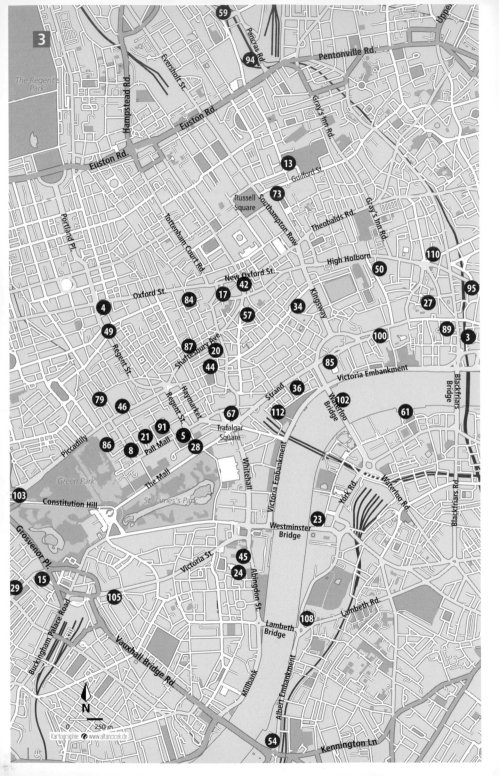

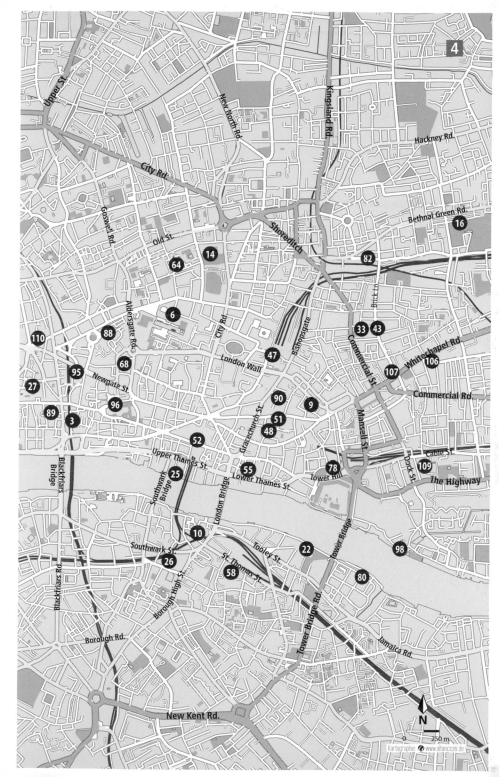

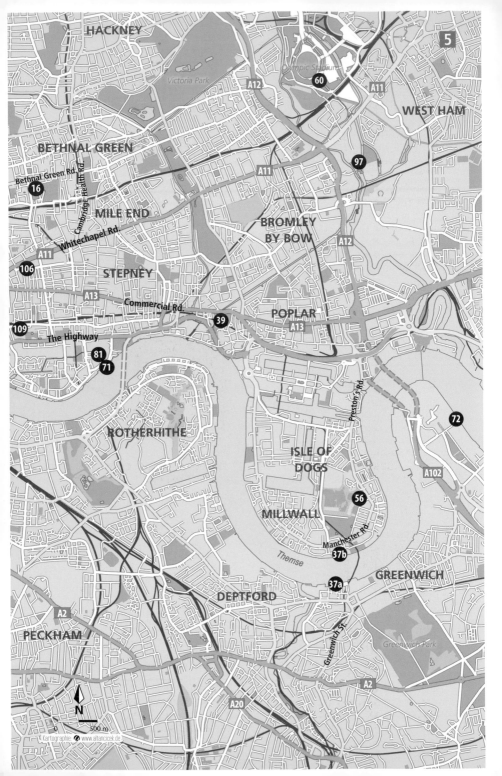

Lucia Jay von Seldeneck,
Carolin Huder, Verena Eidel
**111 PLACES IN BERLIN
THAT YOU SHOULDN'T MISS**
ISBN 978-3-95451-208-9

Rike Wolf
**111 PLACES IN HAMBURG
THAT YOU SHOULDN'T MISS**
ISBN 978-3-95451-234 8

Annett Klingner
**111 PLACES IN ROME
THAT YOU MUST NOT MISS**
ISBN 978-3-95451-386-4

Paul Kohl
**111 PLACES IN BERLIN
ON THE TRAIL OF THE NAZIS**
ISBN 978-3-95451-323-9

Rüdiger Liedtke
**111 PLACES IN MUNICH
THAT YOU SHOULDN'T MISS**
ISBN 978-3-95451-222-5

Dirk Engelhardt
**111 PLACES IN BARCELONA
THAT YOU MUST NOT MISS**
ISBN 978-3-95451-353-6

Peter Eickhoff
**111 PLACES IN VIENNA
THAT YOU SHOULDN'T MISS**
ISBN 978-3-95451-206-5

Ralf Nestmeyer
**111 PLACES IN PROVENCE
THAT YOU MUST NOT MISS**
ISBN 978-3-95451-422-9

Stefan Spath
**111 PLACES IN SALZBURG
THAT YOU SHOULDN'T MISS**
ISBN 978-3-95451-230-0

Marcus X. Schmid
**111 PLACES IN ISTANBUL
THAT YOU MUST NOT MISS**
ISBN 978-3-95451-423-6

Rüdiger Liedtke
**111 PLACES ON MALLORCA
THAT YOU SHOULDN'T MISS**
ISBN 978-3-95451-281-2

Christiane Bröcker, Babette Schröder
**111 PLACES IN STOCKHOLM
THAT YOU MUST NOT MISS**
ISBN 978-3-95451-459-5

Gerd Wolfgang Sievers
**111 PLACES IN VENICE
THAT YOU MUST NOT MISS**
ISBN 978-3-95451-460-1

Jo-Anne Elikann
**111 PLACES IN NEW YORK
THAT YOU MUST NOT MISS**
ISBN 978-3-95451-052-8

Rüdiger Liedtke, Laszlo Trankovits
**111 PLACES IN CAPE TOWN
THAT YOU MUST NOT MISS**
ISBN 978-3-95451-610-0

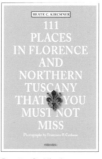

Beate C. Kirchner
**111 PLACES IN FLORENCE
AND NORTHERN TUSCANY
THAT YOU MUST NOT MISS**
ISBN 978-3-95451-613-1

Floriana Petersen
**111 PLACES IN SAN FRANCISCO
THAT YOU MUST NOT MISS**
ISBN 978-3-95451-609-4

Petra Sophia Zimmermann
**111 PLACES IN VERONA AND
LAKE GARDA THAT YOU MUST
NOT MISS**
ISBN 978-3-95451-611-7

Acknowledgements

We are grateful to the following friends who gave us invaluable support during the work on this book: David Brock, Oliver Bryce, Patricia Carroll, Stuart Condie, Maria Ejsmont-Rybicka, André Gren, Jamilla Lord, Simon Lord, Tina Papenfuss, Simon Prior, Ryszard Rybicki, Caryl Varty, Larissa Weeke.

The author

John Sykes was born in Southport, Lancashire, studied in Oxford and Manchester and lived in London before moving to Germany and making his home in Cologne. He has written and translated books about London, including one in the form of a Sherlock Holmes mystery, and is the author of several travel guides about the British Isles.

The photographer

Birgit Weber, born in Menden in Germany, studied in Aachen and lives in Cologne. She has provided illustrations and photographs for a number of books, and has edited travel guides to London. For more than 20 years she has regularly visited Britain, and loves London for its cultural diversity and its mix of historical and modern oddities.